Together
in
Solitude

Together in Solitude

Douglas V. Steere

Crossroad · New York

1982

ACKNOWLEDGMENTS

"Common Frontiers in Catholic and Non-Catholic Spirituality" first appeared in *Worship* magazine as "Common Frontiers in Catholic and Protestant Spirituality," reprinted here with permission of The Liturgical Press, Saint John's Abbey, Collegeville, Minnesota.

"The Life of Prayer as the Ground of Unity" first appeared in *Worship* magazine as "Prayer as the Ground of Unity," reprinted here with permission of The Liturgical Press, Saint John's Abbey, Collegeville, Minnesota.

"Solitude and Prayer" first appeared in *Worship* magazine, reprinted here with permission of The Liturgical Press, Saint John's Abbey, Collegeville, Minnesota.

1982
The Crossroad Publishing Company
575 Lexington Avenue, New York, NY 10022

Printed in the United States of America

Library of Congress Cataloging in Publication Data

Steere, Douglas Van, 1901-
   Together in solitude.

   1. Contemplation.   2. Spiritual life—Quaker
authors.   3. Asceticism.   4. Solitude.   I. Title.
BV5091.C7S74   1982   248.3'4   82–14918
ISBN 0–8245–0531–X

Contents

Introduction   vii

Part One · *Together*   *1*

ONE · Common Frontiers in Catholic
and Non-Catholic Spirituality   3

TWO · The Life of Prayer as the Ground of Unity   18

THREE · On Confirming the Deepest Thing in Another   31

FOUR · Baron von Hügel as Spiritual Director   41

Part Two · **In Solitude**   77

FIVE · Bethlehem Revisited   79

SIX · Solitude and Prayer   89

SEVEN · Contemplation and Leisure   105

EIGHT · The Mystical Experience   129

NINE · On Being Present Where You Are   158

CONCLUSION · Spiritual Renewal in Our Time   179

Introduction

This book was prepared in response to the generous invitation of my friend, Richard Payne, who asked me to draw together a cluster of things that I have written in these last years that deal with the nurture of the interior life. They were written under different circumstances, but they move freely across the borders of Roman Catholic, Protestant, and Quaker insights. I am an active member of the Religious Society of Friends (Quakers). I first met the Quakers in England during my years as a student at Oxford. I have found in their simple but exacting type of corporate silent worship, their faith and experience of the Presence, and their readiness to follow out concerns in the service of their fellows, an abiding source of challenge, strength and renewal.

I have taught philosophy for a long generation at Haverford College. During that time I have been immeasurably enriched by feasting on the devotional treasures of the Roman Catholic tradition and particularly the writings of Nicholas of Cusa, the Spanish mystics, Pascal, Caussade, Grou, Baron Friedrich von Hügel and Gabriel Marcel. I have also been heartened by the Protestant writings of Lancelot Andrewes, Thomas Traherne, William Law, Soren Kierkegaard, Evelyn Underhill, and Charles Williams, and in the company of my own contemporaries, a group that we charitably called the "Younger Theologians." This was a small gathering made up of men like Paul Tillich, Reinhold and Richard Niebuhr, Amos Wilder, Edwin Aubrey, Wilhelm Pauck, Henry Van Dusen, George Thomas, Roland Bainton, Robert Calhoun, John Mackay, and Joseph Hromadka, who for three decades met together for two long weekends each year and probed each others' minds and spirits.

If I were asked who, out of this long chain of witnesses who have blessed me, were my own most moving mentors, my debt and commitment to ecumenism in its deepest sense would be swiftly evident. For apart from my Quaker guides, Isaac Penington and John Woolman, I would be drawn to name Baron von Hügel, Soren Kierkegaard and Romano Guardini. Each of these men in his own unique way has pointed me to the luminous center. Hosea 2:14 expresses their gift in its having God promise that "I will entice you into the desert and there I will speak to you in the depths of your heart." This realization of our togetherness and of our common requirement of solitude has led to the title of this collection—*Together in Solitude.*

A few words may be in order on the circumstances that drew out each of the chapters of this book.

Chapter One: *Common Frontiers in Catholic and Non-Catholic Spirituality* was written and given, together with half a dozen other papers, at the first meeting in late August, 1965, of what was to become the Ecumenical Institute of Spirituality. It was a trial to see how deeply together we were and what common ground we stood upon. All of these papers were published in a double number of the Roman Catholic journal *Worship.* The demand for more copies led the Liturgical Press of the St. John's Abbey (Benedictine) to issue these papers in 1966 as a paperback entitled *Protestants and Catholics on the Spiritual Life.*

Chapter Two: *Prayer and the Ground of Unity* was given in 1969 at an International Workshop on Ecumenism that was organized by the Catholics in Philadelphia and honored with the presence of Cardinal Willebrans. It appeared later in *Worship.* The paper sought to show our common ground in the life of prayer in which our togetherness can be both deepened and maintained.

Chapter Three: *On Confirming the Deepest Thing in Another* was given at the invitation of the Provincials of the Christian Brothers. It outlines and illustrates the common educational task that confronts Catholics, Protestants and Quakers in their schools where all three feel a concern for a spiritually grounded education.

Chapter Four: *Baron von Hügel as Spiritual Director* is a much longer essay than the earlier chapters. It is a very human biographical picture of a great Roman Catholic ecumenist and scholar who, although of German extraction, was Britain's greatest theologian in the first quarter of this century. He is reappearing again today and will richly reward those who read him. This chapter was written to introduce a book of mine, now long out of print, which sought to select some of von Hügel's finest passages. The book was called *Spiritual Counsel and Letters of Baron von Hügel.* This essay will especially interest those who are concerned with the whole field of spiritual guidance. It contains a section that deals with a case study of spiritual direction in which Evelyn Underhill was guided by von Hügel between the years 1921–1925. Togetherness across all denominational boundaries has seldom been better exhibited than in the life of this great Christian.

Chapter Five: *Bethlehem Revisited* was a Christmas message that carried marks of the Vatican Council II from which I had just returned. It depicts the deeper philosophical and spiritual meaning of the Christmas event and what it calls out in us. *Togetherness* and *Solitude* merge at this point. *Bethlehem Revisited* appeared later as a Pendle Hill pamphlet.

Chapter Six: *Solitude and Prayer* was again written for the Ecumenical Institute of Spirituality in 1980 and appeared later in *Worship.* It is an attempt to penetrate the meaning of solitude and to pierce its many facets to discover its role in furnishing a climate for the life of prayer and for breaking through to the very ground of our being. It concludes with some fresh suggestions of how solitude at its best can be a gateway to a whole new level of solidarity with one's fellows and responsibility for the world we live in.

Chapter Seven: *Contemplation and Leisure* was first published in *Humanitas* in an issue that was devoted to the nature of leisure. It appeared later as a Pendle Hill pamphlet. It analyzes with care the nature of contemplation and treats its whole spectrum, all the way from dealing with the commonest things of life to its mystical pinnacle. It probes the common ground that leisure shares with contemplation when leisure's roots are bared. It is full of anecdote and example.

Chapter Eight: *The Mystical Experience* is the longest and most exacting essay in the book and may be skipped until you are ready for an encounter. It was given in 1966 as one of half a dozen papers at the Hebrew University in Cincinnati. The writers on mysticism in the United States were brought together there as the guests of the University on this special occasion when the leading authority on Jewish mysticism in Israel was being entertained in this country. The paper has an academic ring to it, but it contains some precious passages from the great mystics of the Christian religion who stand *Together in Solitude.*

Chapter Nine: *On Being Present Where You Are* was first given as the annual lecture in Australia to the Yearly Meeting of the Quakers. It is a careful analysis of the nature of presence and of what "being present" means. It is illustrated in a variety of areas of life. Père Caussade's passion for the "sacrament of the present moment," and for the necessity for a Christian to learn how to celebrate this continually, gives something of the flavor of this essay.

Chapter Ten: *Spiritual Renewal in Our Time* was first given as my inaugural address as the Harry Emerson Fosdick guest professor at Union Theological Seminary in New York City in the autumn of 1961. It appeared later as a fresh introductory essay in a double volume of my *On Beginning from Within* and *On Listening to Another* that Harpers brought out in 1962. It searches the dimension of sanctity to find the ground of renewal in the continuous conversion that is forever being drawn out in the active spirituality of both a Christian and the Church to which he or she belongs.

DOUGLAS V. STEERE
Haverford College
August, 1982

PART ONE

Together

ONE

Common Frontiers in Catholic and Non-Catholic Spirituality

Our whole enterprise of ascetic or spiritual theology must always wrestle with a certain inner contradiction. No one has expressed it better than Augustine when he declared that "We come to God by love and not by navigation."

It is possible to become so concerned with trying to chart the navigational routes most suited for quickening the inward life of the people of God that we will be tempted to forget Augustine's warning. Yet Catholic or Protestant or Orthodox, we all face this common paradox. To forget that "we come to God by love" is to forget both prevenient grace, whose pull and lure have initiated our coming, and to forget, too, that in responding to this grace, our own surge of love is not readily predictable or chartable and may vary vastly between persons and traditions and epochs—making the task of the spiritual theologians in the map room almost impossible of accomplishment. For many religious thinkers not only is the task unmananageable because of this complexity, it is also undesirable because it implies that the priority seems to be given to navigational techniques and courses, and not to grace and the spontaneous answers of love. This hints at a succumbing to Pelagianism, to the accent upon justification by works, perhaps even to the personal accumulation of merit by devotional practices, instead of resting all on God's supreme act in the atoning grace of Christ and on a man's spontaneous response as the recipient of redemption.

Almost fifty years ago I had a long visit with Karl Barth in his home in Bonn. I was staying at Maria Laach at the time, and I journeyed in from Andernach for the visit. I spoke of the role of private prayer as a means of putting us into the stream of grace and even spoke of how impressed I had been by the rhythm of the daily Benedictine liturgical cycle as a means of exposing a community to this baptism of grace. Barth repudiated both roles and denied that either had the slightest significance as far as my own, or the monks,' redemption was concerned. He insisted that for himself he knew that he hung suspended between heaven and hell, that the weight of his sins would most certainly sink him to hell, and that only the intervention of the supreme act of grace wrought in Christ would ever be sufficient to lift him and to overcome this terrible gravitational force of his sin. He implied that this act of Jesus Christ was enough, that anything else was utterly irrelevant, and that anyone who wasted his time or trust on these practices was to be pitied.

There are few in classical Protestantism who would be quite as brazen as to put his emphasis as bluntly as Barth did to me. But actually, there is a very strong undercurrent in classical Protestantism that would find in these remarks what they deeply believe; and in the United States, at least, neoorthodoxy has had little time for the devotional side of religion and has often regarded it as specious humbug and self-deception.

What I have been describing is not exclusively a Protestant problem. For extreme Augustinian "Grace-is-all-ism" in either confession would rule out the place for human decision and effort in either the initial experience of redemption, or in the subsequent progressive movement toward the basic reorientation required. The Roman Catholic Church has on at least two conspicuous occasions repudiated such a position in favor of a more moderate attitude. Barth's central affirmation about the need of grace stands, but at the same time, we cannot rest easy with the conclusions he draws from it about the channels that may be the agencies through which that grace may most readily flow.

I have accented this paradox because it is always implicitly present in the Protestant discipline and is a common factor to Protestant and Catholic both. If we were to define ascetic theology as the nurture and deepening of the human responses to the grace that is lavished upon men and women, we should not come far afield. For ascetic or spiritual theology in its final sweep seeks always to make that response more adequate and more complete, and it implicitly assumes Leon Bloy's famous line at the close of *The Woman Who Was Poor* that "man has only one sorrow—not to be a saint"—if we were to define a saint as "one in whom God has more and more his undivided sway."

Implicit, too, in our discipline is a view of the nature of human beings, and it is a view that, in spite of all of our various differences of accent, we might, I believe, agree upon: namely, that as creatures, our loving back to God is spasmodic, inconstant, and anything but continuous, that we require infinite encouragement, and that there must be countless occasions of restoration to an awareness of the constant action of grace. I believe we could also agree in assuming that conversion is continuous and that, in spite of one's intentions, there is no such thing as the total commitment of a person to grace. Instead there are ever new areas in one's life, and in the life of one's time in which one is immersed, that call out for further yielding. "How do I become a Christian when I already am one?" is more than a rhetorical question. All of this means that we are unfinished creatures and nodes of unfinished creation even when we have been drenched with grace, and that we require all the skilled assistance that can be given us in the continuous process of increasing self-surrender and inward abandonment to the grace that the Christian life calls for.

The Dimension of the Unconscious

To indicate in still another fashion the scope of our field, it is challenging to turn to C. G. Jung and to see how he has put the matter of the redeemed or still-to-be redeemed unconscious life of Christians in our time:

> The divine Mediator stands outside as an image, while man remains fragmentary and untouched in the deepest parts of him. . . . It may easily happen, therefore, that a Christian who believes in all the sacred figures is still undeveloped and unchanged in his inmost soul because he has "all God outside" and does not experience Him in the soul. His deciding motives, his ruling interest and impulses do not spring from the sphere of Christianity, but from the unconscious and undeveloped psyche, which is as pagan and archaic as ever. Not the individual alone but the sum total of individual lives

in a people proves the truth of this contention. The great events of the world as planned and executed by man do not breathe the spirit of Christianity but rather of unadorned paganism. These things originate in a psychic condition that has remained archaic and has not been even remotely touched by Christianity. The Church assumes, not altogether without reason, that the fact of having once believed leaves certain traces behind it, but of these traces nothing is to be seen in the march of events. Christian civilization has proved hollow to a terrifying degree: it is all veneer, but the inner man has remained untouched and therefore unchanged. His soul is out of key with his external beliefs; in his soul the Christian has not kept pace with external developments. Yes, everything is to be found outside in image and in word, in Church and Bible, but never inside. Inside reign the archaic gods, supreme as of old: that is to say, the inner correspondence with the outer god-image is undeveloped . . . and therefore has got stuck in heathenism. Christian education has done all that is humanly possible, but it has not been enough. Too few people have experienced the divine image as the inner-most possession of their own souls. Christ only meets them from without, never from within the soul; that is why dark paganism still reigns there.[1]

It will do no good to hedge by ruling out such a statement on the ground that Jung, like all psychotherapists, fails to distinguish between the "psychical" and the "spiritual." Ascetical theology cannot escape the responsibility of examining the deep underwater therapy that may be required to touch these depths that Jung has described: to touch the dream life, or to touch the vital axioms—the principles from which we make our choices. For unless a man's unconscious life is involved in his redemption, how little in him will be permanently altered, how heavy will be the shadow that he casts, and how opaque he will be as a window to transmit this grace to others!

Just as Paul, after his most violent and polemical "Grace-is-all" moments in the Epistle to the Romans, moves over to the kind of conduct that can alone channel that redeemed life, so even the most avid classical Protestant, when you put him to the test, insists that a "forgiven man" who owes his redemption utterly to grace must nevertheless channel that new life and be quickened in that new life through drastic changes in his relations with his fellows and through yielding ever fresh areas in his own life to God, areas that may until then have been withheld. The Epistle of James may be called the epistle of straw,

By Luther

but even classical Protestants have discovered that it is hard to make the bricks of a Christian life if you leave out the straw.

Individual Responsibility

Yet there should be no concealing of our differences of accent in this matter, for Protestantism in general lays more emphasis upon the school of individual responsibility in these matters than Roman Catholicism, and it is highly sensitive to any claims that would declare or even imply that the priest, or the saints, or the virgin, or the institutional church stand as an indispensable intermediary. The mediation of Jesus Christ is the only help required, and the individual Protestant believes that any other mediator is not only superfluous, but is a dangerous intrusion that is not only capable of exploiting the individual person, but that may even rob him of his direct touch with the true source of redeeming grace and of his personal responsibility before it.

There was something very beautiful in Abbot Herwegen's gentle rebuke to me when, as a young professor some thirty years ago, I came to Maria Laach to make a month's spiritual retreat. I asked him for someone to lay out a retreat for me, and he told me I had come to the wrong place, that I should have gone to the Jesuits who believed in individual spiritual pilgrimages. The Benedictines, he pointed out to me, had no hope of salvation by their own prayers or inner yieldings. If they were saved at all, it was as a member of the Benedictine family and all quite unself-consciously as the result of the family *Opus Dei*. He capped it with a fine story of a Benedictine abbot's encounter with a departing visitor, and of the visitor's congratulating him on having an abbey of pious monks. To this, the abbot replied with a tone of sadness that he wished the visitor might have been able to tell him instead that he had a "pious abbey."

As an introduction to the flair and flavor of Benedictinism, these remarks of Abbot Herwegen's were magnificent. But on further thought, they are, in their full significance, less impressive. For unless each monk in that monastery is in growth, unless each monk *is* in his own special way being led to give himself more and more completely to God; in other words, unless the Benedictine house is more than a spiritual beehive, a religious collective where all of the individual responsibility has been transferred to "the family" or to those in spiritual authority who enforce the rules, it may seriously be questioned whether any such cenobitic religious institution may be justified before the standard of the deepest ascetic theology. I know that the best Benedictine thought today would heartily agree with this.

The Quaker Tradition

Even though most Quakers, whose tradition I know better than most non-Catholic practice, consider themselves as a third force in the Catholic-Protestant struggle, they nevertheless share the Protestant accent on individual responsibility in this matter of growth in the response to grace, and they go so far as to insist, in George Fox's words, that "Jesus Christ is come to teach his people himself" and to refer to the Holy Spirit's available guidance to the soul of man in Isaac Penington's words: "There is that near you which will guide you. O wait for it and be sure that ye keep to it."

The classical type of corporate worship among the Quakers has always schooled them in looking for the minimum of outside help in finding, in being bidden by, and in following this ever present Guide. For in its classical form, this corporate worship consists simply of the group gathering in a very plain room devoid of all ornamentation and sitting together for at least an hour in an attitude of prayer, turning inwards and waiting on God. In the course of this meeting for worship, Quakers often experience what they speak of as being "gathered" in the presence of Christ. Their own lives seem to be judged, and areas that require amendment are opened to them. Consciousness of sin and of the fact that "He who shows a man his sin is the same that takes it away" is a frequent experience, and Quakers also know what it is to experience in the meeting the forgiveness of sin and the inward absolution. There are often times in the meeting when there is an inward baptism of thankfulness akin to adoration; times of intercession for persons and situations; times when the gifts are accompanied with tasks to be done, which may even come as specific leadings or concerns; and times of having reservations stripped away and "disponsibilité" and expendability restored. All of these inward experiences of communion and baptism and ordination for work to be done that so often take place in the Quaker meeting for worship are a further confirmation of renewal and guidance in the absence of mediation, even the mediation of the customary outward sacraments. And what Quakers here experience corporately, they often find coming to them privately through the week with a sense of direct guidance that again seeks to draw the implications of the encounter of grace for specific human obligations.

When a seventeenth-century Quaker, John Roberts, was arrested for worshiping in other than the Anglican way, he is reported to have said to Bishop Nicholsen before whom he was brought, "Miserable sinners you find us, and miserable sinners you leave us . . . you must always be doing what you ought not: and leaving undone what you ought to do, and you can never do worse. What use is religion if it does not give a man the power to change and the strength to resist temptation?"

This statement of John Roberts could be the query of a pharisee. Perhaps it was. But it could also be the question put by one who felt profoundly the individual's unmediated accountability to the indwelling Christ for following out the guidance that came to him. It could also be a window through which ascetic theology, whether in Roman Catholic or non-Catholic hands, might view its ultimate task and might in some degree measure its ultimate effectiveness. For if our ultimate task is to nurture the response which individual human beings make to the infinite donation of redemptive grace that draws at their lives, can it do this unless it finally succeeds in quickening this ultimate seed of accountability in the breast of the Christian?

In both the Protestant and Catholic traditions, there dare not be any blunting of the responsibility to listen for and to follow this "bird in the bosom," this "guest we have within us." If, in ascetic theology's guidance in the use of spiritual direction, confession, private and public prayer, fasting, devotional reading, or the service of the poor and the afflicted, it should happen that we dry up or diminish a man's inner responsibility to God in Christ or to his following the direct guidance of the Holy Spirit, and instead increase his dependence on the outward apparatus that we may provide, far from favoring him, we may have permanently crippled and deformed the very center or seed in him that God has bid us to arouse and to encourage. Here is a common element in our heritage that may be something of a norm by which to judge our methods.

It might be instructive to take three areas of ascetic theology that are, I would presume, of central concern to Protestant and Catholic alike, and to examine them both for the common ground and for the differences of accent which they may reveal: 1) spiritual direction, 2) the cultivation of the practice of private prayer, and 3) the encouragement of personal involvement in some acts of costly responsibility for our fellows.

Spiritual Direction

It would seem clear that Catholic and non-Catholic alike must admit the need of adequate personal counsel for those who feel a yearning to put their lives more completely into God's hands. Certainly the monastic life and later the life of the in-the-world orders have demanded this. Since the Catholic renaissance of the sixteenth century, there would seem to have been a vast increase in the Roman Catholic effort to provide this service more and more extensively to the laity who wished it. Francis de Sales, who wrote his *Introduction to the Devout Life* (issued in 1609) specifically for lay people, calls the fourth chapter of the first book of his Christian classic "The necessity of a guide, in order to enter on the path of devotion and make progress therein" and declares, "Do you wish in good earnest to set out on the way to devotion? Seek out some good man to guide and conduct you; it is the admonition of admonitions, 'Although you may search,' says the devout [Teresa of] Avila, 'you will never find out the will of God so assuredly as by the way of this homely obedience, so much recommended and practiced by the men of old.' "[2] Francis de Sales develops this virtue of absolute obedience to a spiritual director and adds, "The guide ought always to be an angel in your eyes . . . do not look upon him as a mere man . . . trust him in God who will favor you and speak to you by means of this man putting into his heart and into his mouth whatsoever shall be requisite for your happiness . . . this friendship must be strong, sweet, holy, sacred, divine and spiritual . . . Pray to God to give you such a one [and] remain constant and do not seek for any others."[3] For Teresa of Avila, obedience was such a condition of opening the way for grace that she once declared, "It is more meritorious to pick up a needle in obedience than to eat and drink nothing but bread and water for a whole year."

From the Protestant side, the role of spiritual direction was from the outset heavily discredited by identifying it with the confessional and with the whole apparatus that grew up around monetary penances and indulgences. In its traditional form, spiritual direction plays almost no prominent role in Protestant practice apart from the only partially reformed Anglican Church where the Caroline divines of the seventeenth century and the Anglo-Catholic movement of the last 130 years have both strongly advised it. A contemporary Anglican authority on ascetic theology, Martin Thornton, says, "Spiritual direction is our greatest pastoral need."[4]

In spite of Protestant neglect, the basic need in this area could never be entirely ignored, and it is interesting to read the large group of personal letters of spiritual counsel that Quakers like Isaac Penington and George Fox wrote, or to read the fascinating spiritual journals that all Quakers were encouraged to set down, in order to see how these were used as guides in a fiercely democratic tradition that would have recoiled from acknowledging any such obedience to another man as Francis de Sales suggests. The Moravians and other German pietists have a similar literature, and some day we may be supplied with enough knowledge about the early Methodist class meetings to see that they played no small role in supplying spiritual guidance. A certain amount of pastoral guidance has, of course, always been present throughout Protestant history, and more recently this has been accentuated with the coming of the tidal wave of psychological counseling that has swept through the Protestant theological seminaries in our time.

It is important to note how wisely our Catholic brothers have distinguished the confession of sins and the direction of souls. Even though both functions have often been carried on by the same priest and with the same parishioner, yet they have been so rightly seen as quite different functions. It would be well if the same distinction could be made by Protestants between a pastor's psychological counseling and the spiritual guidance of souls. For the latter is a program for encouraging increased abandonment to God, and while certainly it is not entirely separable from the counselor's attempt to find "who's the matter with you" or to achieve a remission of obnoxious symptoms and an adjustment to the social situation, yet the goals are anything but identical.

Because Protestanism in general—and this would perhaps even hold for the Anglican community—would find the notion of abject obedience to a spiritual director of the kind described by Teresa of Avila or Francis de Sales too alien to their relation to their clergy, and because the clergy would be neither willing nor in many cases qualified to assume any such role, such types of spiritual direction as we have in Protestantism have often come in much more informal and completely nonauthoritarian contexts: from prayer groups and confraternities; from two lay persons conferring together on their common need; and from pastor to lay person in highly empirical fashion as between two friends engaged in a common quest. The impression which a non-Catholic has of Roman Catholic practice in the matter of spiritual direction, as in all other phases of ascetical theology, is that it is regarded as an adjunct of the sacramental and liturgical structure and authority of the Church. If this impression is correct, then in the case of spiritual direction, the priest, whether he wishes it or not, possesses an authority which creates a certain "Distanz" between him and the parishioner, and, as an officer of the Church, the spiritual direction that he gives is likely to be in terms of the Church's liturgy and its fullest use.

Closely associated with this liturgical context for Roman Catholic spiritual direction (even when one knows well that it belies Catholic theory in the matter) is another impression, namely, that there is a hidden assumption that lingers on the minds of the Roman Catholic clergy that spirituality, if it is to be fully invoked, means a kind of commitment which fully professed men and women may be able to approach, but which life in the world will almost certainly prevent, and therefore it is best to ask little and to expect still less of lay aspirants to a spiritual life.

With a more human and less authoritarian Roman Catholic Church in prospect; with a quickened Roman Catholic concern for laity and their problems, a laity many of whom may not be restored to the supernatural life by liturgy alone; with an even deeper sense of the unique and highly personal character of each situation of personal direction, Roman Catholic and non-Catholic alike are confronted with the necessity for a thorough examination of a nonauthoritarian, empirical, and much more tentative type of spiritual guidance that will nevertheless carry sufficient weight to have it honestly and persistently worked at by the layman. Both of us require a searching to find how this direction can be undertaken with a consciousness that the Holy Spirit is the ultimate spiritual director and that the true spiritual guide will always keep this foremost and see his or her role as trying to work with the soul-friend to see what God is drawing him or her to at this stage in life. This is certainly more than Fox's "Take them to Christ and leave them there," but it is a good deal less than the authority many a spiritual guide even in our own day has been known to assume.

While most Protestants and Catholics would, I presume, admit that spiritual direction is an art rather than a science, and while Protestants find Catholic manuals on the subject seemingly less aware than they should be of the lay person's life in our day, nevertheless the almost complete absence of any real attention to this particular function in Protestant theological seminaries is a reflection of the progressive inward impoverishment of the Protestant tradition in our time and points up how desperately we need help—and how important is our task in this field of spiritual theology.

The evangelically oriented groups who comprise a growing sector of the Protestant world seem to be so absorbed in confronting their people with the message of redemption and mobilizing their converts for witnessing to this message that the stages of further yielding and communion are largely neglected. Thomas Traherne, the seventeenth-century Anglican priest-poet, can speak to all Christians in the *Centuries of Meditation* when he says that to contemplate God's love "in the work of redemption, though that is wonderful" is not all. Still greater, he suggests, is the end for which we are redeemed: a communion with his glory. Perhaps a major focus in the spiritual direction of the future must be in guiding people to make some progress during this life of ours in the practice of communion; for surely Martin Thornton is right when he says, "not to long for progress is to fail in prayer."

Cultivation of the Practice of Private Prayer

Archbishop Temple spoke for Catholic and non-Catholic alike when he said, "What we need more than all else [is] to teach the clergy to be teachers of prayer."[5] Here we would seem to be on common ground. For the cultivation of the practice of private prayer, while again not uninfluenced by our respective public cycles of worship, is nonetheless something that cuts across all of our traditions. If we could express in simple terms the objective of what we were trying to accomplish in the life of prayer, I believe that this common ground might be even more evident. Would it be going too far to suggest that what we are after in the nurture of prayer is a continual condition of prayerfulness, a constant sensitivity to what is really going on? For if grace is continually laying siege to every life; if Pascal was not deceived when he wrote "Jesus shall be in agony until the end of the world," endeavoring to tell us afresh that this costly redemptive process is still going on and is forever drawing at our hearts for our healing, for our reconciliation with God and with each other, and luring us into a sense of unlimited liability for each other, then are not all acts of prayer simply precious devices for mobilizing our uncollected faculties and compelling them to wake up and pay attention, and to join the ranks of what is so costingly and tirelessly already at work?

If we turn to such an aspect as the prayer of intercession and the question is put as to whether intercession could possibly affect the life of someone who did not know that anyone was holding him up in prayer, we very swiftly reveal the condition of our spirituality in this area. Intercessory prayer among non-Catholics is used for a large spectrum of purposes including success in all phases of life not exclusive of worldly affairs; it is widely used by healing groups within the Protestant Churches who put great store by it; and it is used in a kind of simple and unthinking way of trust by our more conservative-minded denominations. I do not believe that I exaggerate, however, when I suggest that none of these groups have thought out an adequate theology or metaphysics of what might be involved in the act of intercession. In the more conventional Protestant denominations, apart from a small group of the devout, it is doubtful if there is any real belief in the efficacy and significance of secret intercessory prayer. Even public prayer that includes such elements is tending to become perfunctory. Most Protestants in this large group would agree that intercessory prayer is efficacious in tendering the one who prays, and most would go further and admit that the one prayed for, if he should be one who is ill, would benefit by this proof that he was not forgotten and that he was an object of concern, provided that he knew that his prayer had been made for him. But to think that there is a realm where intercessory prayer poured out secretly by individual persons or, say, by a closed Carmelite convent of nuns could lower the threshold of the heart to the continuous siege of the Divine Redemptive love, that these prayers matter, that they matter terribly in order to reach situations, persons—and the heart of the world—this, in Protestant terms, and in an intelligently worked out, theologically grounded, and philosophically plausible way, is hard to come by in our world today.

I stress the Protestant situation because I know it best, but I learned at the Vatican Council and through many visits with members of spiritual orders of the Roman Catholic Church that even in that communion where it still remains publicly correct to applaud the contemplative orders who intercede for the sins of the world and who give themselves almost wholly to such prayer, abundant doubts are being cast upon its importance when it comes to the real matter of priorities. The pressure to push the contemplative orders out into the world and to get the monastic orders more and more to commit themselves to what the hard-pressed local bishops and society in general would regard as "useful" activist work is an ever growing one. This would seem to indicate therefore that both confessions face a common problem of shoring up intercessory prayer against erosion and of being compelled to think it through afresh and to state its significance with the greatest skill that we can mobilize. And what has been said of this very revealing type of prayer, namely, that of intercession, holds equally for the whole spectrum of prayer and its effective cultivation amid the Himalayan dispersions of contemporary living.

Personal Involvement in Responsibility for our Fellows

When in 1920 Baron Friedrich von Hügel undertook to direct the spiritual life of Evelyn Underhill (Mrs. Stuart Moore), she was already in middle life, married, and one of Britain's most accomplished writers. The Baron began by insisting that she "visit the poor." These two afternoons a week of immersion in the life of the London poor were not suggested with any primary idea of doing *them* good, but rather of restoring her to a responsible personal relation with the brave, bold, boisterous stream of suffering humanity which makes up

Christ's earthly body. It worked in her case and brought her nearer to people, and in their midst she found Christ.

Much of the spiritual revitalization that has come to those who have taken part in the recent freedom walks and in all kinds of civil rights demonstrations with their physical risk, their rough and tumble days bedded down in Black churches and homes, their spells in jail in company with their Black brothers, has come through this same restoration to a responsible relation with what, until then, was a severed limb of Christ's body. Late in her life Dorothy Day, spending nights in a California jail cheering her companions when they were all arrested for marching in support of Cesar Chavez's farm workers, opened the lives of more than a few who shared this experience. Peace and antinuclear vigils have quickened the lives of countless others. Many Catholics and Protestants have found the nearest they have ever come to sensing what is really meant by abandonment to God has come in such experiences, and they know them as authentic means of kindling the life of God in their souls.

True ascetic theology in all the ages has not been blind to the spiritual direction that Jesus gave to all his future followers in the closing portion of the twenty-fifth chapter of Matthew, and that Francis of Assisi confirmed in the love that he lavished on the inmates of the leper hutch at Rivo Torto. The whole tradition of Catholic charity and of Protestant service has had freshly confirmed for it in every generation that Christ's body is truly to be found among those in need and is meant to be tended there, and that those who would serve him must open their arms to all creation. When Joseph's brethren were given the terms of their receiving further grain to save them and their families from the famine in Israel, they were told that they must produce their younger brother Benjamin, who had remained at home. Joseph is said to have put this into words that God may be speaking to us today: "Except you bring your brother with you, you shall not see my face."

An Irish Catholic pointed out to one of my friends that Quakers worked for the poor but rarely joined them. This may come too close for comfort to our whole Protestant tradition of charity. Roman Catholics have often taken that further step and their train of fearless saints puts us all deeply in their debt as we see what it means to become truly vulnerable and how, when it is done in true abandonment, Christ is seen to live again and miracles break out all over the place.

While much care must be taken to distinguish this type of spiritual discipline from the compulsive but much applauded social activism that it can all too readily degenerate into, surely this third element is one that all of us face as a common element in contemporary spirituality and one that we must come to terms with. Difficult as it may be to guide and to control, it presents any ascetic theology in our time with a laboratory that could provide experiments releasing a whole new level of spiritual power to renew the Church in our time.

Notes

1. C. G. Jung, *Psychology and Alchemy,* pp. IIL.
2. Francis de Sales, *Introduction to the Devout Life,* tr. Allan Ross (London, 1930), p. 10.
3. Ibid.
4. Martin Thornton, *English Spirituality* (London, 1963), p. xiii.
5. F. A. Iremonger, *William Temple* (London, 1948), p. 35.

The Life of Prayer As the Ground of Unity

While ecumenism may have begun by meaning "world-embracing" and was spatial in its designation, like most words, it has not stopped where it began. To most of us it means a movement to overcome barriers of fear, barriers of understanding, and even more importantly, barriers of irresponsibility for each other. And it actually means a whole series of functional undertakings for more effectively carrying out our Christian task in the lives of our own people and in our caring for the world.

Cardinal Cushing liked to tell of his predecessor going out to a small parish near Boston during the depths of the depression and asking the local priest how it was going. The old priest replied, "Terrible, your Eminence, terrible, but thank God it's going even worse with the Protestants." I think we have come a stage beyond that. When Roman Catholics lose a Thomas Merton or an Abbé Pire, we non-Catholics mourn almost as they do. And when they face a mass of resignations from the priesthood or a shrinkage in vocations for the religious orders, we feel it as a blow to us as well. If they produce a saint or a mystic like John XXIII or the Swiss woman mystic, Adrienne von Speyer, we rejoice with them. This is what I mean by overcoming a sense of irresponsibility for each other.

In the latter days of the Algerian liberation struggle, when De Gaulle was trying to bring it to a close but suffered one reverse after another in the negotiations, France's old enemy, Germany, which a generation before would have heartily rejoiced in France's bedevilment, now felt as though these very reverses were happening to her. When I saw this I knew that the European mentality was planted in

Germany soil. This sense, not alone of toleration or of coexistence but of genuine proexistence between us in the ecumenical movement, is, I believe, well on its way. But I believe our friendship is still callow and inexperienced in the deeper, functional implementation of such an aspect of ecumenism, in ways of deepening each other's spiritual lives, of teaching men and women how to pray and how to yield themselves to worship. Until we are able to work and to give freely in such areas, the ground of our unity will be frail indeed.

On Turning Around

Let me develop this a little. I met a friend recently whose wife had been suffering from that kind of Parkinson's disease that produces a condition of rigidity. She had been treated to a course of the new drugs that have been developed. He reported that she was much improved, but that when standing she still could not turn around. In thinking about his description of his wife's condition, it occurred to me that my friend had made a fairly accurate description of our present condition as far as helping each other in this inward area that is so crucial for us all. The new ecumenical drugs that we have taken have loosened us up, have improved the climate of our relations with each other, have even helped us with our chronic condition of the hardening of the categories, but apart from a few sporadic exceptions, we are still not able to produce a climate for turning around, for turning round inwardly, for turning round into the life and power of Christ, and for a deep inward passion to move along together and to listen and to speak and to act for the needs of all men.

I am not talking primarily about grit-in-the-eye matters like mixed marriages or intercommunion, or like sharing one another's long-hoarded bank accounts of honors, of endowments, of buildings, of books, of quality education, of scholars, of regional privilege and public esteem. These are all negotiable and in them we have already made some small beginnings.

The kind of turning around that I mean lies well back of these affairs, although they will all be profoundly affected by whether or not this is taking place. Such different people as Dag Hammarskjöld and Thomas Merton and John Woolman have spoken of it convincingly in their personal lives. Hammarskjold wrote in *Markings:* "At some moment I did answer *Yes* to Someone—or Something—and from that hour I was certain that existence is meaningful and that, therefore, my life, in self-surrender, had a goal."[1]

Thomas Merton, writing of a critical moment when he was on his knees praying in a workingman's church in New York, said:

> It suddenly became clear to me that my whole life was at a crisis. Far more than I could imagine or understand or conceive was now hanging upon a word—a decision of mine. It was a moment of crisis yet interrogation: a moment of searching but a moment of joy. It took me about a minute to collect my thoughts and the grace that had suddenly been planted in my soul, and to adjust the weak eyes of my spirit to its accustomed light, and during the moment my whole life remained suspended on the edge of an abyss; but this time the abyss was an abyss of love and peace, the abyss was God."[2]

An eighteenth-century American Quaker, John Woolman, of Mt. Holly, New Jersey, described in singularly restrained language what this turning around meant to him, for he, too, knew it firsthand: "My heart was tender and often contrite and universal love for my fellow creatures increased in me." In the next line of his *Journal* he adds, significantly, "This will be understood by such as have trodden the same path."[3]

All three of these men were led to this basic turning around by an inner dialogue that in its broadest sense is called *prayer.* Cut off this inner dialogue; let this practice in men's and women's hearts be eroded away by neglect; depreciate it; ridicule it; divert men and women from it; and you greatly lessen the likelihood of the occasion for this very inward turning around. It is the purpose of a religious tradition to encourage and to heighten the expectation that such occasions are both possible and highly relevant. Each of these men had received from his own religious tradition some inkling of the inner way; but for each the experience, when it came, was original and fresh. And it kindled in them a further expectancy for what was to become the critical center for each of them in their respective lives as an international diplomat; a writer, poet and later a Trappist monk; and a New Jersey orchardist and tailor who became deeply involved in helping to abolish the practice of human slavery in the American colonies.

This radical medicine of prayer and contemplation, with its steady drawing and its tendering, its lifting up and its putting down, its singling out and its bringing into focus the ever new decisions with which we are confronted, is a medicine that we must help each other to supply.

The plea for it, which it is the sole purpose of this paper to advance, may give us some clue as to how the ecumenical movement might be fed if, at this point, it could be persuaded to open itself to this inward side of its common life. This inevitably leads to several (what the Quakers would call) queries for each of us and our religious traditions to put to ourselves. Has the degree of ecumenical unity that we have already found deepened our lives of prayer in any significant way? Has it drawn us into any new dimensions of inward yielding? Has it produced any mutations in our way of approach to instruction in prayer or to more transforming dimensions of worship? Has it produced vehicles such as genuinely ecumenical retreats, ecumenical conferences on the inward life, on a lay apostolate relevant to our time, on spiritual direction, on spiritual counseling, on common ventures of devotional literature, or such as sharing each other's inward journeys and the precious records of persons who made them? Has it encouraged us in making common ecumenical approaches to the other great world religions?

Your answer may be an admission that what is being queried here has all too rarely happened. But you may suggest that perhaps this is the wrong expectation; that ecumenism from the very outset was not meant to make us turn around in this way; that only God can do that in response to our opting freely for his way; that ecumenism must not be asked for too much; that it was only meant to remove some Himalayan roadblocks, to set right grievous historical sins of separation and to fulfill the scriptural injunction that if your brother has aught against you, go and put it right and then return to the altar to worship. This argument appears plausible. Yet if we are to be really scriptural, have we *returned* to the altar? Have we deepened our life of prayer? Have we experienced the groundswell of overwhelming love that can come to restored and liberated souls?

I believe that the ecumenical movement will be weighed in the gospel balance by the fruits that it produces, and that in the end these fruits will have far less to do than many surmise with the institutional restructuring that may or may not accompany its development. The real test will be whether it can help to turn us around, can help to deepen our personal and our corporate life of prayer, can increase in us the universal love for our fellow creatures that the gospel ethic interprets in terms of an unlimited liability for one another, and can give us the courage and the imagination to go about its implementation in the world.

Action Clarifies Prayer

I once knew an old Dane named Aage Moller whose word used to be, "The less I pray, the more I pray." His implication was that prayer and action are separated by no cleft and that if one really acts instead of praying, one has done all that is necessary. Walter Hilton, in his fourteenth-century *Scale of Perfection,* speaks of those who adorn Christ's head in prayer but neglect his feet and "let the brethren to decay or perish for want of looking to." He adds: "Surely he will more thank thee and reward thee for the humble washing of his feet . . . than for all the . . . decking . . . his head."

In his colorful figure Hilton says almost precisely what a recent French Quaker servant of God, Marius Grout, has said in speaking of contemplation in our day: "If contemplation, which introduces us to the very heart of creation, does not inflame us with such love that it gives us, together with deep joy, the understanding of the infinite misery of the world, it is a vain kind of contemplation; it is the contemplation of a false God. The sign of true contemplation is charity."

To point out some cleft between the decking of the head in adoration and the washing of the feet, between the vision of prayer and the deed of commitment, is essential. The critics of prayer in our day have fastened here on a legitimate distinction. It may well be, too, that the look of those of us who *do* pray may be for these critics what Nietzsche once said of all the Christians that he had known: "They do not seem to me to have the look of redeemed people." But when we have said this, we have surely another say coming. And it is that prayer does not *always* stop on the vision side of the cleft; and that action, the fruits, have always been a test of Christian prayer. Action has even been an agent of the clarification and the deepening of the original bidding that came in prayer.

I admit freely that there have been some apologists for prayer and even some of the great Christian saints who have at moments complained about their practical occupations interrupting their contemplation of God. Among them are even persons like Bernard of Clairvaux, with his incessant travelling over all of Europe on countless diplomatic errands, or Catherine of Genoa running a busy hospital. Yet Emerson had the word that describes what these very acts of theirs really did for their prayers when he said that only in action "can thought ripen into truth."

Prayer Cleanses Action and Restores Its Frame

But to think that acts alone, even apparently selfless acts, are enough to win justice for the deprived is again to fall into the cleft from the other side. For acts require vision or they themselves become loveless and bitter and lifeless. Che Guevara ruefully kept writing in his diary that he and his men had failed utterly to win the confidence of the Bolivian peasants. They were not able to get a deep enough vision of these peasants as human beings; the peasants instead became for them only stepping stones for their revolutionary designs. It is all very well to relate, as Gollancz does, the Talmudic tale that when Moses struck the dead sea with his wand, nothing happened. The Red Sea opened only when the first man plunged in. But without the frame, the vision, the encouragement that came in the time apart, Moses would never have had the faith even to have led them to the sea. Prayer is the restorer of the frame, the meaning, the restorer of human faces, the inward cleanser of the distortions of action just as action is the clarifier and tester of prayer's real intent and of its genuine commitment.

Many may come into the life of prayer and worship today through disillusionment with action alone, just as the counter culture contemplatives are staggering their way by all kinds of routes to something that will transcend the highly disciplined industrial society, which seems to them to be harnessed to values which they, like the earlier Franciscans in their society, find not worth the effort. Others may be won to it by experiences of decisive action, by moments when they are swept beyond themselves. And still others may be drawn to pause when they find that at last they belong to mankind by having identified themselves with groups which until now they have never even faintly understood.

For those determined to take the nonviolent approach both to help the deprived find their way to put a floor under their poverty and to lessen the disparity in income, health, longevity, and educational opportunities, prayer becomes an even more indispensable agency towards recovering the center of strength and love for both the deprived and for those cast in the role of the depriver. For without this center of renewal there can be little hope of resisting the temptations to drop back into the violent way, and to help to build up the walls of hatred and contempt that the future will inherit for its destruction. Not by accident did Jesus resist those temptations in the desert and their repetition almost every day of his life.

Action continues to crave a frame of meaning, to require a living cambium layer through which the sap may flow up from the roots and refresh the tree of one's life. As an agency of the deepest humanity, man is not likely to be deprived of prayer for long. Yet to the vast throng of people, even in our own ranks, prayer must be reinterpreted and must be seen as a part of the built-in equipment of one who would come to his or her full stature in all relationships. Thanks to God's infinite patience and to the creative passion in men for music and poetry and drama, there is still a base from which to work. If ecumenism shirks this task, it has little future.

Catholic, Protestant, Jew—in this matter of prayer we are all at the same frontier. None of us suffers from any delusion of adequacy. What are we then to say to each other about the life of prayer and the ground of unity? What is there to say about prayer in our time, in any time? Augustine, sitting down to write the eleventh book of the *Confessions,* on the nature of time, says frankly: "If you don't ask me, I know, but if you ask me, I don't know." How true this is of prayer!

Augustine, however, speaks for us all and goes to the heart of what happens in true prayer and worship when he says: "I was collected from the dispersion in which I turned from thee, the One, and was vainly divided." How better than in terms of dispersion could we describe the condition today of overactive man? Yet how much easier it is to describe the uncollected, overactive man than to describe in any detail the collected man or the means of his being collected.

Prayer is a principal agency of collection from dispersion. It rouses us not only from the Gethsemane sleep where we fail our Lord. It rouses us, too, from the condition of somnambulism, the uneasy sleepwalking in which so many of us stagger through our lives in this world, never really there to our families, to our children, our friends, our colleagues, our neighbors in need, even though we may think that we are feverishly busy, supposedly in their interest.

To pray is to pay attention to the deepest thing that we know. Quakers use the words *center down* to describe the human voluntary act, and the word *gathered* to express the further involuntary dimension of what often, though not always, happens in a real season of prayer. As this paying attention takes place, this centering down, this being collected, this being gathered, our awareness expands. We are made awake: awake to our finitude, awake to the great gulf stream of love that will not let us go, awake to what each relationship in which we stand really means, sometimes overwhelmed with despair at our past insensitiveness, but cleansed, refreshed and renewed in hope by what has been opened to us.

Prayer intensifies us. It wakens the sleeper in us and restores a thankful heart. And a thankful-hearted man opens the hearts of those about him. His sense of creatureliness, which prayer continually renews, makes him thankful to return to the human race, able to laugh at himself and his pretensions, and able to be of use in all kinds of situations. I think this is what my friend David Jenkins means when he gathers up all he has to say on prayer in a single sentence: "Prayer is a space in which to become truly human."

There is a Senegalese proverb that says that when God sends opportunities he does not, for all that, wake up the sleeper. The sleeper may, in fact, be most strenuously engaged in active good works. He may be so active that he has forgotten the danger where "even those who wished to help, wished also to direct"; or where the philanthropic impulse when uncoiled reads, "We are all here on earth to help others; but what on earth others are here for, I don't really know." To even the most active of us the words may be spoken: "They are the dead who do not know they sleep." Seeds of the innovative, the really new opportunity, and the opening of the way for it to enter the situation in which I stand often come in prayer and in the attentiveness that it nurtures. It is this which the Cologne philosopher Peter Wust must have meant when, as he lay dying, he concluded: "The greatest things are only given to those who pray." Professor A. N. Whitehead speaks of inward religion as "an offensive against the repetitive mechanism of the universe." How often the man of prayer opens the pores of the universe to something new.

William Temple in his *Nature, Man and God,* following closely along the lines of Alfred N. Whitehead's process philosophy, goes so far as to suggest that these God-given opportunities, these inward charisms, these fresh and new nudgings and biddings in the existential situations in which each of us stands (for which our African friends insist: do not wake up the sleeper) may be critical moments for the whole thrust of cosmic redemption. This means that if we sleep on in overactivity and underattention and smother these biddings in favor of the universe's repetitive mechanisms—the customary expectations which we have of each other, the rigidities in our relationships, the hopelessness and despair of any lasting or significant changes that sabotage positive measures for their unlimbering—then God's whole strategy may have to be altered.

William Temple insists that while the ultimate nature of God is unchanging, his strategy is infinitely variable. Whether, then, I am asleep or am so anesthetized in activity that these openings never waken me; or whether, if they do come, I drowsily reject them in favor of the repetitive mechanisms of the universe, has not only personal, but cosmic consequences.

God the Iconoclast

The profound psychologist of the soul, Blaise Pascal, declares in his *Pensées* that in every man "there is an infinite abyss that can only be filled by an infinite and immutable object, that is to say, only by God himself." And to be sure, in such an insight as this he is describing another discovery which persistent prayer brings to us as a costly gift. When the safe, tidy, not-likely-to-change-much icon that I have formulated of myself, of who I am, confronts in prayer the secure, well-domesticated icon of God that, once again, I have projected on the All-in-All, most people do not expect much that is startling to happen. But if prayer and worship are really undertaken seriously, then one day, quite unexpectedly perhaps, in some stripping situation of life or perhaps in some moment of pause, I may suddenly find that the boundary lines I have set to both of these icons of mine have been swept away, and that the until-now undisclosed abyss of mystery in me and the transforming abyss of mystery in the One I confront have suddenly met. And the involvement is so profound that it compels me to reassess all that I have known until now. C. S. Lewis, speaking of real prayer in *Letters to Malcolm,* says it well:

> Only God himself can let the bucket down into the depths in us. And on the other side he must constantly work as the inconoclast. Every idea of him we form, he must in mercy shatter. The most blessed result of prayer would be to rise thinking, "But I never knew before, I never dreamed. . . ." I suppose it was at such a moment that Thomas Aquinas said of all his own theology: "It reminds me of straw."[4]

Listen to how a contemporary Dane, the late Anker Larsen, describes this experience:

> I had been sitting in the garden working and had just finished. That afternoon I was to go to Copenhagen, but it was still an hour and a half before the departure of the train. The weather was beautiful, the air clear and pure. I lighted a cigar and sat down. . . . I just sat there. Then it began to come, that infinite tenderness, which is purer and deeper than that of lovers, or of a father toward his child. It was in me, but it also came to me, as the air came to my lungs. As usual the breathing became sober and reverent, became as it were incorporeal; I inhaled the tenderness. Needless to say the cigar went out. I did not cast it away like a sin. I simply had no use for it!
>
> This deep tenderness which I felt, first within myself and then even stronger around and above me . . . drew me into the Eternal Now. That was my first actual meeting with Reality; because such is the real life: a Now that *is* and a Now which *happens* . . . . I sat in my garden but there was no place in the world where I was not.

A few pages later, he declares:

> "If I had all the food in the world in one dish, all the wine in the world in one glass, all its tobacco in one cigar. . . . and the promise in addition that I should have all these things continuously, if only I were willing to renounce the possibility of experiencing again those meetings with the Eternal Now, and the illumination of life that they would bring—I would laugh heartily and throw the whole collection of trinkets on the dunghill. If I have forgotten anything

else one might covet, I throw it after the rest without looking at
it.[5]

The fruits of the opening of our inward lens to this deeper awareness spill over to nature and strip away "the veil of familiarity from
things." George Fox declared, "The whole creation has a new smell."

Yet even deeper, this Christian contemplation may plunge us into
the world's misery and make us expendable. It often girds us to go
on with our small part in ministering to it even when we feel we have
already done our share and more. When Teresa of Avila staggered in
the task set her, she was told in prayer, "Now is not the time to rest."

My wife and I slipped into the St. Benedict's chapel at Rosettenville
in Johannesburg early one morning and found the Anglican priest,
Trevor Huddleston, who wrote *Naught For Your Comfort,* lying face
down in prayer before the altar, gathering strength for the day in his
struggles for the African cause. Where would Archbishop Helder
Camara be without the continued bidding and renewal that comes
from the inward vigils?

New Dimensions in Ecumenical Experience

In closing I simply mention the stimulus which a small group of
Roman Catholic and non-Catholic writers in the field of prayer and
the inward nurture of the spirit have given each other in intimate visits
together ranging from four to eight days. We have been probing each
other's traditions on the common problems of the inward life. We
swiftly came to learn that our divisions of opinion seldom ran along
the lines of divisions of faith, but that a Benedictine and a Quaker
might be defending the contemplative tradition against the attacks of
two Catholic activists! None of us will ever be able to write anything
again without the witness and insights of the others as a very part of
his own mind and spirit.

A few brave attempts at ecumenical retreats have been made by the
Gustave Weigel Society and other agencies, but we are still groping
in the dark as to how to deal firmly and effectively in these ventures.
We still are shy about reading each other's devotional treasures. All
of us are tyrannized by a haunting feeling that psychiatrists have
largely taken away the role of personal counseling from the clergy,

and that we need to discover the new dimension they have disclosed and to bring it into the deeper levels of spiritual direction.

Aelred Graham and the late Thomas Merton have done much in this country to draw attention to the contemplative tools of Hinduism, with its immense experience in concentration, and of Zen Buddhism, in its use of the rigorous habit of Oriental meditation as an aid to help release an almost irrepressible surge of spontaneity in its members. They have encouraged us in our contemplative poverty to scrutinize these with care and to see how we may learn from each other. Merton declares:

> "I need not add that I think that we have now reached a stage (long overdue) of religious maturity at which it may be possible for some-one to remain perfectly faithful to a Christian and Western (monastic) commitment, and yet to learn in depth from, say, a Buddhist discipline and experience. I believe that some of us need to do this in order to improve the quality of our own monastic life and even to help in the task of monastic renewal which has to be undertaken within the Western Church.[6]

In an ecumenical colloquium carried on in Japanese in 1967 between ten Christian scholars (Catholic, Protestant, Quaker) and ten outstanding Zen Buddhist masters and teachers, we were deeply impressed when Fr. Enomiya Lasalle, for fourteen years Jesuit provincial in Japan, told at some length how Zen breathing, bodily posture and meditative practices, which he had carried on for almost two decades, had rekindled a dead and burnt-out Ignatian prayer life and given him a whole fresh life of Christian prayer and devotion.

When a Japanese Zen Buddhist master asks a Quaker how in a single weekly hour of public meditation he can keep himself centered down and refreshed for all that he does in the week, the query goes on ringing in the ears. When a French Canadian Roman Catholic asks a Quaker how he gets along without the habitual reminder of Jesus Christ's presence that he himself finds in the corporate mass, this too goes on resonating long after the friend has gone his way. When a Hindu lives in an American Protestant home for a month and asks his host when is the time in the day that he takes for the healing of the soul, this is ecumenical crossfire that is not easily shaken off.

We need each other: each other's traditions, each other's queries, each other's faithfulness, each other's accents on elements we have neglected, each other's encouragement, each other's heroic saints, each other's confessions of failure and longing. Where Roman Catholics and Orthodox seem to those of us in the freer traditions to be far too fixated on overstructuring the processes of prayer, we Quakers may well seem to be specialists in collective woolgathering in our outwardly unguided movement into the presence of God. How we need this gentle nudging of each other within the fellowship of the ecumenical movement! For if we can find ways to help each other to become more deeply established at the center, we may dare to be ever so much freer in our decisions about conflicting issues at the periphery.

The life of prayer as the ground of unity—I remember the words of an old Frenchman that are said to have been spoken at Verdun after almost countless months of agony and frustration: "There are no hopeless situations. There are only men and women who have grown hopeless about them." I have no despair over the human spirit and the unquenchable hunger which will drive us back to the source that can alone sustain and cleanse and renew us. Dare we across all of the lines of our religious groups be among those who may help to call out this hunger in each other? Dare we not only listen to lectures on prayer but be prepared to go into the laboratory as well? If God is where we let him in, and prayer and worship are proven ways to lower the threshold to his entrance, may we in closing be encouraged by a contemporary who gave as his blessing, "Not in your strength, or your skill, but in your need may you be blessed."

Notes

1. (New York: Knopf, 1964), p. 205.
2. See Edward E. Rice, *The Man in the Sycamore Tree* (New York: Doubleday, 1970).
3. John Woolman's *Journal,* Whittier edition, pp. 58–59.
4. (New York: Harcourt, Brace and World, 1964), p. 84.
5. *With the Door Open* (New York: Macmillan, 1931), pp. 72–73, 82-83.
6. The author's reference is to an unspecified piece by Merton on monastic experience and East-West dialogue.

THREE

On Confirming the Deepest Thing in Another

In looking at the spiritual task of education today in schools that are avowedly guided by religious groups who are concerned that they offer something that is distinctive, I believe there are certain basics that they apply at all levels of the educational task. I think that those who care enough about this kind of education to foot the costly bill for their children to have it, are going to be increasingly selective and demanding that something unique be given, and it is in this setting that I will try to share a few reflections on what I think constitutes that unique and infinitely precious climate that such schools at their best may be able to provide.

As for the teachers in such schools, I am assuming at the outset that these teachers have at least a strong beginning of competence in the field in which they are to teach. There is no place for incompetence in the religiously rooted educational institution of tomorrow. These institutions will be smaller. They will be chosen and not imposed on parents. The days of "take it or leave it" are over. Incompetence can no longer be hidden as it could in the older authoritarian structures. But after saying this, I must link it to the confession that the question of what will constitute competence in a teacher in the religiously concerned school of tomorrow and how you form and how you choose such teachers is no easy matter to fathom!

Obviously, such a teacher must be saturated with a personal interest in his or her field if it is to be contagious. In certain earlier situations of teaching, there were built-in safeguards that would swiftly eliminate teachers who lacked contagion. I have visited the old Al Azhar University in Cairo that began in the tenth century A.D. This university began on a mosque porch where a man who had something to teach would appear and spread his rug or blanket on the floor of the porch, and interested students would come and sit down around him. If he was interesting, they would remain for months or perhaps years listening to his wisdom and exchanging views with him. If he was not, they simply got up and left him, and a dull or incompetent teacher ended up with an empty rug! The medieval Christian university in Europe was little different, for students went from teacher to teacher, and the ones who were saturated with their subject and had important things to say held their students. In these situations there were built-in controls for handling the matter of competence and a capacity to communicate.

When I think of the great teachers that I have personally known, men like Bliss Perry, Alfred North Whitehead, Mark Van Doren, Paul Tillich, Reinhold Niebuhr or my late colleague, Rufus Jones, they have all, in their teaching, seemed to be confiding things that you had already dimly sensed yourself, but they did it in such a way as to give you glimpses of so much more and of such new levels of meaning that even if they mystified you with their further dimensions of insight, they lured you on.

I have always liked Lincoln Steffens' suggestion in his *Autobiography* that when opening a subject for a student, the teacher might do well to tell him, first of all, of some of the unsolved problems in the field that are still to be tackled and to give him a sense of how little is known, and how many things there are to which he himself might be able to make some significant contribution to their understanding. The genuine humility of such an approach introduces a note of integrity and of openness into the student-teacher relationship from the very outset. At college level, I forsee that we shall some day reach a point where the insignia of rank of professor and student may disappear, and in its place there may emerge only junior and senior fellows at work on the problems in the field.

I have found that it seemed to be an encouragement to men beginning the study of philosophy to remind them that two of the great British empiricists, Berkeley and Hume, at their age already had sketched out in their jottings in the journals or day-books the full outline of all that their later philosophy was to depict in developed form; and to note that their own fresh insights and the queries that they found themselves setting to each of the problems these men focussed upon were highly important and might bring out fresh angles that had never been accented in precisely this fashion before.

I have long been an admirer of still another great teacher whom I did not mention earlier, namely of Martin Buber. I cannot think of a better way to introduce another quality of an inwardly centered teacher than to describe an incident that took place over twenty years ago at Haverford College. In about 1950, I had heard that Martin Buber expected to be in the United States for a visit and had arranged for him to be a guest for several days at Haverford College almost immediately after his arrival from Israel. I had secretly hoped that he might inspire the faculty as well as the students by his insights and by the example of his skill as a teacher.

In those days, each Thursday, late in the morning, we had half an hour when the whole college, faculty and students, crossed a little bridge and trooped up a blocklong path to the Quaker Meeting House where we sat together in a religious exercise based on corporate silence. Martin Buber walked over to the Meeting House with me, and on the way I explained to him the Quaker way of breaking the silence with a brief message if the Spirit quickened him to do it. I explained that no one would formally invite him, that no message was expected from him, but that if something came to him that he wanted to share with the four hundred students and staff gathered there, that he might simply rise and share it and then sit down again and the silence would continue. He told me that he had been in some Quaker meetings in London and knew the procedure, but assured me that as a guest, he would never dream of breaking the silence. I said that this was fine but that I simply wanted him to know the way of proceeding.

The meeting convened and after ten minutes or so Gilbert White, the President of the College, rose and spoke of what a great thing it was that people could meet each other across barriers of race, of nationality, of economic status, of age and could reach out and touch each other. He amplified this by several telling illustrations. He had barely sat down when Martin Buber rose in his place, looking with his beard and his strong face and piercing eyes much as I would picture one of the Old Testament prophets, and after leisurely taking in the whole group with his eyes, he began to speak. He told us that it was a great thing to transcend barriers and to meet another human being, but that *meeting* another across a barrier was not the greatest thing that one man could do for another. There was still something greater. The greatest thing, he continued, that any man could do for another was to *confirm* the deepest thing he has within him. After this, he sat down as abruptly as he had risen. There was little more to say. And there is little more to say about the greatest thing that a teacher can do for a student. He can believe in him; he can have faith, especially at times when all the conventional indicators point the other way in the student; and he can confirm the deepest thing the student has within him.

Anthony Bloom, a leading Russian Orthodox man of the spirit who lives in London, tells, in an autobiographical chapter that introduces a recent book of his, of an experience that he counts as the initial quickening of the spiritual core in him.

> I was sent to a boy's summer camp when I was about eleven years old and there I met a priest who must have been about thirty. Something about him struck me—he had love to spare for everyone and his love wasn't conditioned by whether we were good and it never changed when we were bad. It was an unconditioned ability to love. I had never met this in my life before. I had been loved at home but I found it natural. I had friends too, and that was natural, but I had never met this kind of love. At the time I didn't trace it to anything. I just found this man extremely puzzling and extremely loveable. . . . This experience I think was the first deep spiritual experience I ever had.

It might be well to remember that for a teacher it may be easier to do this for a bright student than for one who is not in the ninety-ninth percentile! How important it is to recall that the greatest spiritual genius in France in the nineteenth century was probably the Curé D'Ars, and that he was apparently a D– student by any respectable French academic pattern of measurement. I have always been touched by Martin Buber's telling us somewhere that early in his career as a teacher in Jerusalem, he selected only the top students academically for his limited-sized classes. Later he took students as they came and found it much more satisfactory. I suspect that a teacher who can take what God gives him and find the center in each that needs confirming, is the most acceptable to God. How many men and women can point back to a teacher who saw and believed in them when they neither saw nor believed in this deepest thing in themselves, and can witness to its decisiveness in their own self discovery and subsequent life quest? The teacher did not put the deepest thing there. It was there already. But he confirmed it.

Thomas Kelly was a colleague of mine in teaching philosophy at Haverford College for almost five years until his sudden death in 1941 at the age of forty-seven. His *Testament of Devotion,* which is a devotional classic of the flavor of Brother Lawrence's *The Practice of the Presence of God,* has been translated into a number of languages and has been widely read. After his own college years in a small Midwestern college, he spent the year of 1913–14 at Haverford College where he came as a graduate student to study under Rufus Jones. He came to Dr. Jones's study during the first week of his time at Haverford, and in the course of their visit, he blurted out, "I want to make my life a miracle." Instead of cutting him down to size or passing this over as a young man's emotional extravagance, Rufus Jones quietly confirmed this deepest longing in Thomas Kelly, and before his life span was out, he *did* become a miracle—a miracle that long after his death is still moving many of his readers to confront the one thing needful. Every student, like every man or woman, has this same secret longing to have his life a miracle. A teacher of real faith and humility is often able to nurture and to confirm this secret longing. At Rufus Jones's memorial service in 1948, a former student of his put it all in four words, "He lit my candle."

I personally owe everything to such a man who taught English Literature at the agricultural college that I attended in Michigan. I never took a course from him, but he became my friend, and in a critical year, he was expendable in time and in confidence, and he confirmed in me a decision to leave agriculture and move into philosophy about which I knew almost nothing in any formal sense. But far more than helping me in this drastic vocational shift, he trusted me and he helped bring back my faith in my having something to give.

Many sincere and able teachers in religiously concerned educational institutions have times when they feel that a kind of invisible barrier has swept in like a cloud of fog from the sea and has cut them off from their students. They find their own religious tradition in which they have felt secure being ruthlessly searched by their students who seem no longer even to start from the teacher's presuppositions. Some of these teachers have found not only comfort but penetration of this cloudy barrier when they have seen the concern that these very students have shown not only for lifting the curtain of pain and injustice in near and distant places, but for their yearning for great music, for the drama, for the creative arts, for the crafts and very especially for nature. Paul Tillich did much to call attention to the significance for true religion that belongs in the operative presence of this depth dimension in man, a dimension which our Roman Catholic brothers have often referred to as "general Revelation." Tillich sensed this depth dimension in Jungian psychology's pointing beyond the empirical or "Who's Who" self to a healing, integrative core or ground that can draw persons back to health if they can reestablish creative relations with it. He found it in painting and saw mirrored in Picasso's *Guernica* a vision of the "brokenness" of modern man in his unredeemed condition. Late in his life, he was fascinated with the depth levels of consciousness that his Zen Buddhist friends revealed to him. He would have been the first to reassure religiously oriented teachers that as long as you have this depth dimension in so many areas operating in your men and women, you have a threshold, a living layer of spiritual seeking to learn from and to confront. This may in the end by a far more fruitful condition of the soul to speak to with great literature and philosophy and history, than the so-called previous ages of faith when the lid was on and all things were more tidily in their appointed places!

When I invited Martin Buber to Haverford College in 1950, I mentioned before that I had the faculty as well as the students in mind. For only when the faculty are in growth and are learning from each other and learning from the students and are continually rethinking their approach to their field can you possibly have a maximal climate for learning to take place all across the board in the school. I knew that Martin Buber had had a small and intimate circle in Frankfurt which met for an evening each week and which two of my German friends had testified was an electrifying experience and one that searched them to their depths. I had always hoped for some American equivalent of this, perhaps at Haverford, and during Buber's visit to a sizable group of the faculty one afternoon, I sought to draw from him the secret of this Frankfort group's intense and continuing aliveness. He thought for a time and then exploded with a single word, *Rucksichtslosigkeit*—this is, to follow the argument ruthlessly wherever it goes, with no holds barred, and with a determination to press through to the full truth involved. This all-out honesty with each other, he felt kept the way open for experiences of new insight and truth to break through.

This experience with Buber recalls in my mind a similar circle around Theodore Haecker in Munich that kindled its members and had rich results. It also makes me think of a small band of secondary school teachers who were gathered together by Georg Picht during the years he was headmaster of the Birkelhofschule at Hinterzarten in the Black Forest. Georg Picht chose these men of course for their abilities in teaching the various subjects in the humanities. But he also made sure of their proficiency in Greek and their keenness in cooperating in a joint project of producing a Plato Dictionary. These men taught their various subjects with a great abandon in the school by day, but nights and weekends and vacations, they worked like beavers on this Plato Dictionary and found the experience both fascinating and exhilarating and found it quickening the whole sweep of their teaching and their educational enterprise. I must add one more example of this kind of teacher collaboration in an exciting project. It centered around Rudolf Steiner and the famous Waldorfschule in Stuttgart. Before the first World War Steiner had drawn together a sizable group of German people in a fresh and very free religious movement called Anthroposophy. Toward the close of the war his followers demanded that a school be set up for their children and that Steiner, this religious genius, should fashion a fresh pedagogy that would guide the school and help to prepare the children for the life-stance of their religion.

Steiner went to work and by the close of the war he had produced a series of highly innovative practices for a new school. There was to be handcraft for the elementary school children from the very first grade; eurythmics were devised to set the body free. Sympathetic biology (agriculture) was set up so that in proper season the children worked daily in large gardens greeting the plants with love and restoring their own connections with the earth. Modelling in clay was introduced further on in the curriculum which then moved into sculpturing in which often deep inward conflicts were worked through in the fashioning of a series of heads. Painting and toy-making were not neglected. The teachers in the school were believers in this approach. There was a rigorous form of self-selection operative since the school was only able to pay the teachers about a half of what they would earn in a state school. But the side benefits were inestimable, for each week these teachers gathered for a seminar with Rudolf Steiner, who had devised the pedagogy. The session began when school closed at three and no terminal hour was set! In this weekly seminar the teaching experiences of the week were pooled, failures were probed, and fresh approaches explored. When teachers in a school or college are themselves in growth something spills over into their teaching that is unmistakable.

The kindling and rekindling of the teachers becomes more likely when there is a growing sense of the urgency of certain tasks that are to be faced and the sense that the stakes in this matter of the task are high. John Hersey, in his documentary novel *Hiroshima,* describes the atomic bomb explosion in the center of the city of Hiroshima and the incineration of those within the immediate range of the bomb. In the same instant, houses in the further ranges of the bomb's perimeter were collapsed, and many people trapped under rafters and beams were unable to extricate themselves and faced the horror of the fires spreading everywhere.

The universal impulse was to flee the city toward the country, and the streets were crowded with hurrying people. Hersey tells of the agonized cries of imprisoned people pinned down in these collapsed houses calling out for help and of these hurrying crowds seemingly utterly oblivious of anyone but themselves. Hersey suggests that most in the crowd seemed to be too self-absorbed in their own survival even to hear the cries. He adds, however, that there were others who certainly heard those cries but partitioned themselves off from touching any center of responsibility by assuming that the police, the army, or the Japanese equivalent of the Red Cross corps would take care of them. But this is not all. Hersey goes on to speak of how here and there, some hurrying refugee would hear a cry, would drop out of the crowd, pick his way into the collapsed building, and give a hand to releasing the trapped person and helping him to escape. Teachers in religiously guided schools and colleges in the period in which we live must face the issue of how you produce this third type of effectively compassionate people: people who hear, people who refuse to run for cover in assigning the task to institutional agencies, and people who are not afraid to drop out of line to respond to the need. For Christian education with its Gospel story of the Jericho Road as a pivotal parable in their great tradition, cannot shrug off the "Hiroshima problem."

Arthur Gossip, a much revered Scottish Protestant minister, tells of how he came to the late afternoon of an exhausting day visiting his parishioners in a working district of Glasgow and at four o'clock stood at the foot of a five-story tenement building where one of his parishioners lived on the top floor. He said that he was feeling exhausted and said to himself, "I'll go home now, and come back tomorrow." At that point, a vision of a pair of stooped grey shoulders started slowly up the steps and a voice seemed to say, "Then I'll have to go alone." He concluded, "We went together."

How in the educational experience of the young in our schools we can provide climates of expectancy and self-abandonment is the task laid on a teacher in a religiously concerned school and one that we dare not evade. It is no good brushing aside this responsibility by insisting that the whole social system that permits wars and atomic bombs and permits Glasgow tenements must be changed. The men and women who will work tirelessly for those lasting changes must know this inward center where they dare leave the crowd or where they dare mount the steps of need regardless of the self-preservative substances that sluice through their blood streams.

What the voluntary work camps of the past generation provided in the way of exposure to the urgent needs of deprived people, both domestically and abroad, and the deep satisfactions to be found in some of the small steps to remedy conditions in which their own bodies (Franciscan-like) were involved, must become a part of the total educational process and would, if it were woven into it, do much to temper the lassitude and boredom of sixteen years of bookish education.

It was deeply confirming to me to attend a conference of the Deans and a number of the leading professors of the Eastern and Midwestern medical schools some years ago and to find them wrestling with the steady deterioration of the sense of social responsibility in their medical students as they passed through the three years of their medical school training. They had checked this with a very carefully devised set of sociological tests and it showed that each year the social responsibility quotient of the medical student in training went a sizable notch further down. There was only one leading medical school where the score bucked the tide. This school was found to expose its medical students to hospital rounds with bed patients from their very first months of entering the medical school. Apparently the close and existential personal touch with the sick had a quickening turn to the Hiroshima "third way" or the Glasgow stair-mounting decisions and it altered their score from the trend of those students who had only theoretical instruction until their very concluding semesters! How close all of this is to getting at the motivational springs of education in both teacher and student about which we know so little but which religiously concerned schools, if they have any real justification, simply dare not neglect.

I will close this cluster of reflections about the teacher and his role in a religiously concerned educational institution by sharing with you a word of one of our great teachers in the past generation, Columbia's Mark Van Doren, whose long career there as a teacher of literature has left its stamp on our time. I once got him to come to Haverford to address a banquet given to a group of a hundred young men collected from our neighboring institutions and our own college who showed high intellectual promise and whom we hoped to interest in considering college teaching as a professional career. Near the close of his address, Mark Van Doren told this group that when he took hold of the doorknob of his own classroom to enter it for his lectures, he always paused. It was holy ground, a holy opportunity! Would he be able to measure up to it? Can we be given the grace to help to share in this anticipatory awe? Einstein says that "he who can no longer stand wrapt in awe and wonder is no longer alive." Can our profession be helped to recover a larger measure of this aliveness?

FOUR

Baron von Hügel
as Spiritual Director

Baron Friedrich von Hügel was in himself a kind of European ecumenical movement. He was born in 1852 in Florence, the eldest child of a late marriage between a mature Austrian diplomat, Baron Karl von Hügel, who was serving as Austrian Ambassador to the court of Tuscany, and a beautiful young Scottish girl not yet twenty, who was the daughter of General Farquharson. After seven years of service in Italy, his father became Ambassador to Belgium, and the son spent the next seven years in a French-Flemish civilization with his education largely directed by two Germans, one a Catholic diplomat and historian, and the other a Protestant pastor. Upon his father's retirement, the family moved to Torquay in England where a Quaker, William Pengelly, opened to him the world of geology. As a result of this remarkable education, von Hügel for the rest of his life was not only completely at home in German, Italian, French and English, to say nothing of Latin, Greek, and Hebrew, but as a Roman Catholic, he was able to speak with great understanding to the Protestant mind of his generation.

When he was twenty-one, Friedrich von Hügel married Lady Mary, the daughter of Sidney Herbert, a member of Gladstone's Cabinet, and three daughters were born to them. Von Hügel inherited a small income from his father, which with modest living was enough to meet his family's needs. A generous slice of it was always reserved for charity. This situation set him free to give himself to the life of the scholar and counselor without the dispersion of an outside vocation.

Apart from some nine winters spent in Rome where he was in the closest contact with Vatican scholars and officials, he lived his whole adult life in England and his books were all written in English. Having inherited from his father his title as a Baron of the Holy Roman Empire, he remained an Austrian citizen until the outbreak of the first World War.

Von Hügel first made his scholarly reputation through scientific biblical papers, but the enormous theological and philosophical learning which he assembled quietly over thirty years in his capacity as a private scholar was no secret to the best British men of letters who sat with him, first in the Synthetic Society and later in what became almost his personal passion, the London Society for the Study of Religion. It would be hard to overestimate what these two intellectual clubs meant to the mutual stimulation of the members in their work. Just as, a generation before, the best German spiritual culture was hammered out and nurtured in the passionate weekly or fortnightly meetings in some café around a Martin Buber in Frankfurt or a Theodore Haecker in Munich, so these London gatherings in their lively although somewhat more moderate exchanges furnished a climate of growth that von Hügel and his distinguished comrades cherished. "Baron von Hügel was our Greatest Theologian . . ."

When his great two-volume *Mystical Element of Religion* on which he had worked for twelve years finally appeared in 1908, von Hügel, like Kant at the appearance of the first *Critique,* was in his middle fifties. From this time until his death in 1925, von Hügel became acknowledged in Britain as doyen of the theological and religious writers of his generation. This reputation was further confirmed by the appearance in 1913 of his *Eternal Life* and in 1921 of the first volume of his *Essays and Addresses on the Philosophy of Religion.* The second series of *Essays* and *Addresses,* the *Selected Letters,* and *The Reality of God* were published posthumously and these went even further in underlining von Hügel's standing in his generation. Dean William Inge, who was not especially given to fulsome praise, once wrote of him, "Baron von Hügel was our greatest theologian and the ablest apologist for Christianity in our time."

Unlike John Henry Newman, von Hügel as a Roman Catholic layman held no official position in the Church. Yet apart from Newman, in the century from 1825–1925, it would be hard to find a figure in Britain to compare with von Hügel either in stature or in influence on Protestant and Catholic alike. He numbered his scholarly friends from both confessions and from both Britain and the continent, and his vast correspondence was written freely by hand in French, German, Italian, or English to suit the convenience of the receiver. In Germany there were Protestants like Troeltsch and Holtzmann; in France, Catholic men of letters like Loisy, Blondel, Brémond and Laberthonnièrre; in Italy, Duschène, Murri and Fogazzaro; in Sweden, Archbishop Söderblom. In Britain itself he exerted a profound personal influence on men and women like George Tyrrell, Maude Petre, C. C. J. Webb, A. E. Taylor, Norman Kemp Smith, Evelyn Underhill, Dean Inge, and Claude Montefiore, to name only a few.

This rare and astonishing gift for friendship, and for the kind of friendship that engages with the ideas of another, often took the form of letters to a writer whom von Hügel had "discovered" in which he expressed his deep indebtedness for some freshly expressed insight. No one will ever know what these letters of discriminating encouragement meant to the recipients. Left very deaf by a bout of typhus fever in his early manhood, von Hügel found it easier to write letters than to see visitors, but personal visits were far from excluded, and at his home in London he was host to a wide range of Christian seekers.

Von Hügel's Own Debt to Spiritual Guides

He felt that in any spiritual counsel he could share, he was only repaying in a small way what had been lavished on him at two great crises in his life, one in late adolescence and another at a kind of spiritual climacteric at the age of forty, by spiritual guides of great wisdom. These men had helped him to move on into a life of increasing self-abandonment to God within the life and station in which he stood.

In 1910 he wrote a letter to Emelia Fogelklou, a Swedish Quaker friend of mine, telling her what he owed to these two men:

> My own conversion came through, or on the occasion of, my first
> sacramental confession when a precocious, wholesome, much-complicated soul of (turned) fifteen. It was deepened appreciably when
> at eighteen by the, to me, utterly unforgettable example, silent
> influence, and definite teaching of a mystically minded but scholastically trained Dutch Dominican [Father Raymond Hocking] in
> Vienna when I was sickening with typhus fever, when my father had

just died, and when "the world" which till then had looked so brilliant to me, turned out so distant, cold, shallow. And the final depth attained so far was mediated for me at forty. I felt at the time and feel still that it came straight from God, yet on the occasion of and by the help of man—by a physically suffering, spiritually aboundingly helpful, mystical saint, a French secular priest [Abbé Huvelin] dead now since only a year.[1]

Ten years later, he passed on to his niece Gwendolyn Greene, a flash of what the first guide had taught him.

When at eighteen, I made up my mind to go into moral and religious training, the great soul and mind who took me in hand—a noble Dominican—warned me—"you want to grow in virtue, to serve God, to love Christ? Well, you will grow in and attain these things if you will make them a slow and sure, an utterly real, mountain-step plod and ascent, willing to have to camp for weeks in spiritual desolation, darkness and emptiness at different stages in your march and growth. All demand for constant light, all attempt at eliminating or minimizing the cross and trial, is so much soft folly and puerile trifling." And what Father Hocking taught me as to spirituality is, of course, also true, in its way, of all study worthy of the name.[2]

In his *Eternal Life,* von Hügel speaks of what the second guide, the Abbé Huvelin, had taught him about the service of one soul to another:

There is before my mind with all the vividness resulting from direct personal intercourse and deep spiritual obligations, the figure of the Abbé Huvelin . . . a gentleman by birth and breeding, a distinguished Hellenist, a man of exquisitely piercing, humourous mind, he could readily have become a great editor or interpreter of Greek philosophical or patristic texts, or a remarkable Church historian. But this deep and heroic personality deliberately preferred "to write in souls," whilst occupying, during thirty-five years, a supernumerary, unpaid post in a large Parisian parish. There, suffering from gout in the eyes and brain, and usually lying prone in a darkened room, he served souls with the supreme authority of self-oblivious love, and brought light and purity and peace to countless troubled, sorrowing or sinful souls. . . . In the *Conferences on Some of the Spiritual Guides of the Seventeenth Century,* Huvelin once declared,

"God who might have created us directly, employs for this work, our parents, to whom He joins us by the tenderest ties. He could also save us directly, but He saves us, in fact, by means of certain souls, which have received the spiritual life before ourselves, and which communicate it to us, because they love us."[3]

A Theology of Spiritual Guidance

It is quite impossible to understand von Hügel and his service to his generation without giving full weight to the ideal which these men had visited upon his mind and to the vision which they had opened to him about his own ultimate vocation. It is my own personal conviction that this service of spiritual counsel on the part of von Hügel was not, as some of his family regarded it, an incidental avocation or an intrusion that sapped away much energy and attention from his theological and philosophical writing. On the contrary, this service of spiritual counseling was the central axis that even set the frames for his intellectual contribution. For that reason, when we come at last to assess the significance of the contribution of this religious giant, I believe that it will be as a guide and encourager of souls that he will be chiefly remembered.

Von Hügel's philosophical and theological contributions are of immense suggestiveness. His monumental study of *The Mystical Element of Religion* is in its depth without parallel in our century. In the course of developing a highly tenable theory of religious realism in *Eternal Life,* in *The Reality of God* and, in a more casual way, in his two volumes of *Essays and Addresses on the Philosophy of Religion,* he recovered for the Anglo-Saxon religious world the dimension of transcendence in the Christian faith and thus did much to correct a current strain of subjectively tilted psychologism in liberal religion. In Britain, at least, this also did much to spare it from the long and debilitating hangover that would almost certainly have followed if British religion had been compelled to receive this corrective by means of a rebottled import of continental Barthianism. I remember Canon Streeter remarking one day how thankful he was that British religion had received this accent on the transcendent from von Hügel instead of Barth, and adding wryly, "We shall one day have so much less to unlearn."

Finally von Hügel's witness to the significance of corporate worship and to the historical and institutional side of religion came with peculiar timeliness and weight to a generation of liberal free churchmen whose offerings leaned in the direction of moralistic preaching and who regarded the Church primarily as a convenient "pulpit" from which to speak.

There needs to be no minimizing of the significance of these theological and philosophical thrusts of Baron von Hügel for the life of our time, when it is nevertheless asserted that the impact of his writing will in the long run be felt in its genius as a spiritual witness to the encompassing reality of God and to its power in encouraging the nurture that men and women require in order to grow in their awareness of that encompassment and to respond appropriately to it. It is striking what confirmation of this assessment one gets as he notes how quaintly von Hügel's books are studded with passages that do not belong in the precise and measured assaying of a religious problem. In the least likely places in his writings, there flames forth a burst of witness or an admonition that seems only to be focused on guidance of the spiritual life of the reader.

Adoration and Religious Realism

His insistence in personal counsel, for example, that religion is adoration, and that any approach to religion that ignores the adoration of God is "like a triangle with one side left out" gives the clue to a major factor in his rejection of idealism in favor of a form of religious realism. This philosophical scaffolding of realism, of an admission that there is a vast givenness in God which we encounter, which we apprehend but never fully comprehend, which penetrates us, which stirs our organs to response, and yet which always preserves its abyss of mystery in the very course of quickening our souls—what is this but a description of a kind of stance by which the soul is poised and directed toward the Object of adoration? The guide of souls, knowing that a soul must adore if it is to grow into an awareness of encompassment, has sketched a rough philosophical diagram that shows how this interpretation of the soul's relationship to God sheds illumination on the act of religious growth at the same time that it provides a crude philosophical road map which serves for the other areas of life experience as well. The goal of his philosophical and theological thought is always identical. It is to give a clue to the breathing space the soul requires if it is to slip the tightly knotted bands of self-serving and move into the heroic self-spending company of the servants of God.

The Requirements of a Full Religious Ration

The same focus upon the guidance of souls is seen in von Hügel's highly plausible account of the three elements in religion that is expanded in the first eighty pages of his *Mystical Element of Religion.* Here a full and fruitful religion is described as containing a creative tension between the mystical or emotional element, the historical or institutional element, and the intellectual or scientific element. If religious practice attempts to delete or to neglect the critical scrutiny of the intellectual and scientific element of religion, it not only weighs itself down with superstitious accretions, outdated cultural patterns, and often with uncriticized ethical practices of a spurious character, but it is powerless to engage fully with the thought of the generation in which it lives in order to express to them in viable terms the truth it longs to share.

If religious practice should seek to omit or write off as "enthusiasm" the mystical and emotional element in religion, in favor of some rigid intellectual or ethical formula or in an effort to preserve intact some set of traditional institutional forms, then the elegant heating plant stands as frigid and useless as an automatic oil furnace when a storm has cut off the current.

If in the burst of an enlightenment period, religious practice seeks to live on intellect or science alone, or in a romantic age to exist on an exclusive, inward focus upon the mystical and emotional element of religion, scorning the historical element with its witness to an historical revelation and turning its back on its institutional counterpart, the Church, then once again impoverishment results and that healthy staple of sound Christian religion, a deep sense of "creatureliness," dries up and disappears. This neglect of the historical and institutional element in religion often produces side effects, anemic aberrations in the form of synthetically fabricated intellectual and scientific religions or of the emaciated and twisted stereotypes and patterns of emotional religion, neither of which is crossed and humbled and fructified by some corporate transmission of a great normative revelation.

On a corporate scale where these personal tendencies are written large, it is not difficult to see the thrust of von Hügel's analysis in Unitarianism where the intellectual and ethical have been to the fore, or in Quakerism where the mystical and the intellectual have been favored over the historical, or in the Roman Catholic Church where, in the modernist struggle in which von Hügel was deeply involved, the historical-institutional was being exalted over the intellectual and scientific. Yet here, at bottom, von Hügel is once again giving a formula for the guidance of souls and insisting that the full response to the encompassing reality must draw the soul to prize the fruitful tension of all three of these elements operating in it simultaneously, and that it will ignore any of them only at its peril.

The spiritual guide who will speak to the soul's real need must teach it the place of each of these elements in a full religious diet or ration. He must cultivate the inner mystical life through the practice of private and corporate prayer and worship. The spiritual guide must also meet the terrible gravity-like pull of sin in that one he is guiding by the historical revelation of God's redemptive power in Jesus Christ. In full awareness of the shortness of man's memory, he must make sure that there is no neglect of the historical and institutional element that serves as a constant reminder of man's calling and of his redemption, and which in the course of kindling in him an unlimited liability for others, enlists him as a member of a great company of the living and the dead who are involved in this redemption of the cosmos. And finally, the guide of souls must encourage the educated seeker in a deep and abiding respect for the intellectual and the scientific element and in the latter case seek even to suggest, at least in an amateur way, the practice of some objective scientific pursuit so that the purifying, other-directed discipline of scientific objectivity may chasten and scarify the almost universal predisposition to self-absorption. All is a laying of a framework within which a guidance of individual souls may be most effectively carried out.

The Nature of Religious Truth and the Nurture of Souls

In his reaction against the arrogant finality of the stiff, hard, geometrical pattern of scholastic distinctions as applied to the deepest reality of all, it is hard once again not to see the guide of souls at work. Speaking of this scholastic tendency in the elder Wilfred Ward's mind, in a letter which he wrote to Algar Thorold on August 15, 1921, von Hügel declared:

> I believe men's minds to be largely, perhaps all, classable according as they act as follows: they instinctively push out to the margins of things and there they remain restless and dissatisfied unless and until they there perceive or think they perceive, clear lines of demarcation. Such minds see truth, reality of all kinds—or what they take to be such—as so many geometrical figures: within these luminous lines all is true, "safe," "correct," outside them at once begins error, "danger," incorrectness. Such was W. G. Ward's mind—at least as he willed and worked that it should be. Then there are other minds which see truth's realities as intensely luminous centres, with a semi-illuminated outer margin, and then another and another, till all shades off into outer darkness. Such minds are not in the least perturbed by each having to stammer and to stumble. When they have moved out some distance, they fall back upon their central light. They become perturbed really, only if and when minds of the geometrical type will force them for the time into their own approach and apprehension.

This kind of insight and flexibility in dealing with theological distinctions points once more to von Hügel's extraordinary flexibility in understanding souls of very different types who all need broadening and deepening if they are to resist the business of a too early firming up, and yet souls each of which has a bent that must be reckoned with and helped to bring its particular gift to the service of truth.

Whether it is the treatment of the problem of the relation of God to evil and suffering, or the yearning for immortality in man, or of the experience of nature and of the ordinary responses of the senses, of the creation of an object of art, of the achievement of a moral victory as witnessing in a preliminary way to the continual operation upon man of a Greater than himself, the same accent is to be seen. Without any interpolation whatever, von Hügel's humble handling of the problem is immediately translatable to the guidance of souls who are faced with both the daily fabric of life and with life's extremities.

There is no intention here of suggesting that von Hügel is a kind of religious pragmatist who is satisfied with any resolution of a problem that will bring a smooth and swift anesthesia to an aching heart. The younger Wilfred Ward wrote von Hügel in the early nineties that what he prized in him very especially was his refusal to oversimplify religion. Instead he presented religion in all of its stark complexity and mystery and yet as lighted up by a faith in its power to transform men and to fashion out of them a company of the highest characters that human history has ever known. It was only by helping man face what *is,* that von Hügel felt he could ever be stirred to move outward to what *ought to be* and not vice versa. Yet the bent of mind of von Hügel never leaves out of sight for a moment the object of his quest: namely, to minister to the hungering souls of men.

If it should be queried whether this is not the ultimate aim of all sound theology, the answer called for would seem to be a thumping affirmative. This does not, however, wipe out either the distinction or the accent that has just been explored. For in most of what passes for theology it would only be with considerable homiletic skill that a distillate of the implications for the guidance of souls could be obtained, and there might well be elements of the theological position which when so applied to human guidance would turn out to be literally destructive of the hope of souls. The devout evangelical Christian humanism of von Hügel, on the other hand, moves back and forth between the revelation of God in the Christian tradition and the condition and needs of the soul like a weaving shuttle, and while there is no claim that he has ever presented a fully articulated system of theology, the problems he has touched upon are always approached in this fashion and his contribution to them would seem finally to be accented heavily in this direction.

Von Hügel's Qualifications as a Spiritual Director

Von Hügel had at least four signal gifts as a spiritual director. In the first instance, he was saturated with an awareness that God was at work, that he is present and operative and laying siege to every soul before, during, and after any spiritual director might come upon the scene. He loved to quote Bernard of Clairvaux on the prevenience of God where Bernard is speaking of a Cistercian monk who thought he could get into the place of prayer before God was there.

> Do you awake? Well, he too is awake. If you rise in the night time, if you anticipate to your utmost your earliest awaking, you will already find Him waking, you will never anticipate His own awakeness. In such an intercourse you will always be rash if you attribute any priority, any predominant share to yourself; for He loves both more than you love, and before you love at all.[4]

Von Hügel himself knew what it was to be a needy one. "People often ask me what religion is for," he confided to his niece. "I simply cannot get on without it. I must have it to moderate me, to water me down, to make me possible. I am so claimful, so self-occupied, so intense. I want everything my own way."[5] Breakdowns, shattering disappointments, personal suffering, long spells of dryness, these he had known at first hand, and in his extremity he had found what a firmly rooted spiritual counselor like Raymond Hocking or Huvelin could do to help bring his life back into its true focus again. Von Hügel not only bore in his own flesh the scars of past need but this was the kind of need that returned continually. "I Need Thee Every Hour" was not a sentimental hymn to von Hügel. Hence his constant personal dependence upon daily religious practice inoculated him against any underestimation of the magnitude of the resistance in men and women to the growing self-abandonment which the interior life requires. He knew, too, how swiftly a life could be impoverished that either neglected or felt that it had passed beyond the staple remedies that have been given men and women for countering the relentless downward pull of the worldly adhesions of the soul.

In addition to these two qualifications, he also had a profound reverence for the differences in souls. "Never forget the enormous variety of souls," he warned his niece. He had experienced the costly failure of his early attempt to throw his own pattern and concerns upon his gifted elder daughter, Gertrud, and had been painfully liberated from the shriveling but widely pervasive temptation that haunts a director, that of regarding his own religious experience as normative, and of seeking to shape all souls like his own. "One is enough," Emerson warned a teacher who sought to stamp his pupils with his own signet, and the thrust of the punster's "One man's Mede is another man's Persian" seemed to distinguish every step in von Hügel's mature approach to spiritual guidance. He quoted with gusto the final sentence of Fredrick William Faber's lecture on Ignatius of Loyola. "This then, my dear brethren, is St. Ignatius' way to heaven: and thank God, it is not the only way."[6]

To his niece Gwendolyn Greene he gave the following counsel:

> The golden rule is to help those we love to escape from us
> . . . Souls are never mere dittos. The souls thus helped are mostly
> at quite different stages from our own, or they have a quite different
> *attrait.* We must be tolerant and patient, too, with these we can and
> ought to help. This difference in souls wakes us up, and makes us
> more sensitive and perceptive.[7]

Finally, von Hügel was himself expendable in the business of guiding souls. There seemed little or no sense of self-preservation left in him and he gave himself without reserve to those whom he believed God had sent to him for help. With at most a working capacity of only two or three hours a day, because of his frailty in the closing years of his life, with his "brain-fag, an old friend," his extreme deafness, his frequent "white nights" where he shared the insomnia of God, with his growing obligations for essays and addresses at important occasions that culminated in the great honor of the invitation to deliver a set of the Gifford Lectures, he still found time to lavish on persons like Gwendolyn Greene and Evelyn Underhill the richest treasure of counsel that he could mobilize. Moreover, they were continually in his prayers. "Three times a day, I pray for you."

He wrote to Evelyn Underhill in 1921, four years before his death:

> One little word more. Do not, I pray you, if ever you feel at all
> clearly that I could help you in any way—even if by only silently
> listening to such trouble and complications as God may send you—
> do not because I am busy, shrink from coming to me, or letting me
> come to you. We are *both* busy, so we have each the guarantee that
> we will not take up each other's time without good cause. But such
> good cause arising, it would, it will be nothing but consolation for
> me, if you let me help as much as ever you feel the need. I will pray
> my little best for you, that God may bless and keep you along this
> path—so safe and so sound—and which (at least in time) will bring

you consolations of a depth and richness far surpassing the old ones.[8]

Without in any way contradicting what has been said above about von Hügel's humility before the ultimate mystery and uniqueness of the souls of those he guided, it is equally clear that his expendability was such that if he thought that any experience that had come to him would be helpful to another, he was not restrained for an instant by any false reticence or fear of disclosing his own personal humiliation or weakness from sharing it freely with the one he was guiding. Yet all of this was done with a delicate readiness and even positive suggestion that it be laid aside or rejected if it was not immediately helpful.

His niece wrote of this quality: "He lived in a deep interior world where few, perhaps, can follow—giving himself to an interior life; tearing, as it were, out of himself great chunks of truth and bringing them to the surface, explaining to us what we can gather and understand."[9] In another place, she records his own counsel to her about what to do with these "chunks." "Leave out all that does not help you. Take only what you can and what helps. Wipe your feet on my old hair, if it will help you, my little old thing."[10]

A Case Study in Spiritual Direction

Perhaps the most effective way of seeing von Hügel at work as a director of souls would be to take a specific instance and look into it carefully enough to indicate some of the characteristics of his method of approach.

In 1921, after a good deal of reflection, Evelyn Underhill (Mrs. Stuart Moore) asked Friedrich von Hügel to act as a spiritual guide for her. She was in her middle forties and von Hügel was approaching seventy. She was an Anglican and von Hügel a Roman Catholic. Both were acknowledged intellectual leaders in the British religious circle of their day. She had known von Hügel for over ten years and during a part of this time had had a number of personal visits with him. She sensed that with all of his great gifts for friendship, he was not easy at the immanentist foundations of her faith nor at her interpretation of Christian spiritual life in her *Mysticism* (1911) and subsequently in the row of volumes that had followed it.

It was not her first experience with a Roman Catholic spiritual guide. After a time of spiritual renewal that lifted her out of agnosticism, and before her marriage, which took place in her middle thirties, she had consulted Father Robert Hugh Benson and by 1909 had been on the point of being taken into the Roman Catholic Church. The rugged objection of her lawyer fiancé and the heavy hand of the Roman Church's antimodernist oath that had appeared at just that point, had restrained her from taking the step.

Now in 1921, some twelve years later, she had once again had an unexpected flood of spiritual renewal. The war years had taken their spiritual toll, and had left her inwardly dispersed. Outwardly, apart from the shock of the death of her beloved friend, Ethel Barker, everything seemed coming her way. She was happily married. She had a circle of unusually intimate and devoted friends. She was secure and "even petted," as she put it, in her professional life, and as a writer on religion she enjoyed the somewhat flattering experience of having a growing number of people who wrote to her for spiritual help. Yet this latter circumstance had, as always, its barb within it. For the growing reliance upon her for help brought with it a growing doubt in her that her spiritual foundation was strong enough even to carry her own life, let alone to nurture others. With her uncannily shrewd power of self-analysis, she had her hunch where the trouble lay. She knew that she was given to strong antipathies, and that one of them was for the institutional aspect of religion. This led to her minimizing the historical and sacramental element in religion and to a pressing of the mystical, experiential element as overwhelming decisive. She also knew that in her own practice of the Christian religion, any personal attachment to Christ seemed to her sentimental and unreal and she knew, too, that the theocentric approach in prayer and worship was her natural bent.

Curriculum for a School of Sanctity

Still more deeply, from her touch with the great souls of Christian history and from this utterly undeserved and unexpected surge of the forgiving love of God that had lifted her up out of the dispersion in which in the war years she had, in Augustine's words, "turned from Thee the One and been vainly divided," she knew that she was marked for sanctity. But she knew equally well how much in her and in her extremely well-adjusted life resisted this call, how much might have to go, and that without stronger help and guidance than she could herself provide she would almost certainly sink back on the outward assurances and fail both God and those who looked to her for help. For the friend who wrote von Hügel for aid had, as most seekers have done, come a long way toward clarification before she ever sought his help and direction. Then as now, these hunches, these intimations, these preliminary clarifications may still be ever so evanescent, and ever so readily lost. What they need is the confirmation, establishment, and sinking of roots, the challenging and rephrasing in the face of the challenge which can so often by effected only by going over them again before God in the presence of another. Hence the call for help.

Von Hügel's reply to her had about it the feeling of the entire naturalness of one Christian coming to another in this way. He once told his niece, "One torch lights another. . . . It is best to learn from others; it gives a touch of creatureliness," and in his reply to Evelyn Underhill he does not seem surprised at all, but only expresses his deep thankfulness and confirmation of what is beginning to come clear to her.

> You evidently realized why and where I was hoping and praying for a development in you . . . what I directly and clearly wanted for you was just what you now tell me you have gained and won! Deo Gratias. I congratulate you and beg you to persevere most faithfully in all that is positive in this your new and, I pray, confirmed outlook. Of course you will have dryness, disgust, strong inclinations to revert to the more or less pure "mysticism." But it is excellent news that, preparing one of these addresses for Manchester College, Oxford, you found that you had really come out strongly and self-committingly for Traditional, Institutional, Sacramental Religion.[11]

The next letter, which followed on this one, where he had confirmed her hunch that she must recover for her own religious life and interpretation the centrality of the institutional element, contains a strong word of caution about pressing this new insight too far, too fast. He notes the operation of a kind of Boyle's law in the spiritual world that tends to make the intoxication with the most recent discovery result in an almost inevitably violent depreciation of all states that immediately preceded it, and writes, "As a matter of fact I fear for you as much the over-doing of institutionalism as the ignoring or even flying from it: indeed these two extremes are twin sisters in such a soul as yours."[12] He follows this by a minimal institutional program for her own personal nurture, yet one that he encourages her to stick to through times of consolation and desolation without much alteration: one church service on Sunday, preferably the early communion in her own Anglican church, and a mid-week visit to an early convent service in a house which is well known to her.

He trails this cautiously by a further reservation: "Perhaps even these two practices are too much for the minimum, since, of course, not the resolution alone but the execution matters really, and I should wish to save you above all things, from any real overburdening."[13] Here he is seen fitting his counsel to a high-strung person who, while in less danger than most of substituting religiosity for religion, might very well be overburdened by the institutional and be driven into a subsequent revulsion for it. Then he lays down for private devotions her "deliberate praying," a maximum of half an hour a day for prayer together with a three- to five-minute examination of conscience at night before retiring. The prayerful disposition that penetrates all she does is the one unrationable blessing in which he encourages her.

Some Laboratory Proposals

One religious retreat a year seems in order to him and it may be of several days' duration, but he warns her against membership in any religious guild or order at this stage. He characteristically suggests the cultivation of some nonreligious interest such as music, painting or gardening. To all of this, he adds a major suggestion of two afternoons a week to be devoted to "visiting the poor." This final prescription he suggests will do more than anything that he can propose to thaw out the cerebral accent in her religion and to break open her heart to the needs of all. In the course of doing this, it may help her to realize increasingly how little her sophisticated religion is able to speak to the needs of these people.

I believe you ought to get yourself, gently and gradually, interested

in the poor; that you should visit them, very quietly and unostenta-
tiously, with as little incorporation as possible into Visiting Socie-
ties, etc. You badly want de-intellectualizing or at least developing
homely human sense and spirit dispositions and activities . . . it will,
if properly entered into and persevered with, discipline, mortify,
deepen and quiet you. It will, as it were, distribute your blood—
some of your blood—away from your brain, where too much is
lodged at present. And if and when religion does appear on the
scene, you will find how homely, how much of sense as well as spirit
it has and had to be. Again, how excellent for you! For what is a
religion which cannot mean anything to the uneducated poor?
. . . I would carefully give preference to the two weekly visitations
of the poor above everything else, excepting definite home and
family duties, or any express wishes of your husband—in each case
as distinct from your own likes and dislikes.[14]

He does not cut her off entirely from her own work of spiritually
counseling others, but suggests the wisdom of cutting it down for the
immediate future and of avoiding taking on new cases.

On the matter of her very deep emotional involvement in her friendships with women, he suggests that these may be a compensation for
the overintellectual character of her theocentric religion and that if
this religion could broaden its base, some of this craving for these
possessive friendships might abate. He counsels a gentle detachment
within attachment, a holding of these persons up to God and keeping
this Ground of friendship always to the fore.

More important than any of this, however, would seem to have been
von Hügel's effort to get her to face the neglected share of the incarnational aspect in her religious life: of what Jesus Christ was and what
he revealed about God, and to get this into the warp and woof of her
thought and practice. He knew from her books that she was no
theosophist, that in addition to the theocentric approach there was a
deep respect for what Jesus Christ had brought into the world. But
beyond a distant respect and admiration, he found none of it either
in the frames of thought in which she was interpreting the Christian
religion or in her personal life of prayer.

In seeing the director of souls at work at this point, there is first
of all no forcing. With such a commanding mind as hers, it is clear
to him that she must face the main issue and not bypass it, if she is

to move at all. It is only what she is convinced really is, and not what ought to be, that can ultimately hold her. He seeks first of all to get her consent to the proposition that at least some Historical Happenings are necessary to the Christian religion. He notes that she occasionally writes as if the Christian religion would be entirely unaffected if all these Historical Happenings were shown to be false. He asks for a decision on this ambiguity in her approach and suggests that she consider whether the time has not come "gradually but most thoroughly" to drop this nonhistorical attitude. This step taken, he asks if she is prepared to see in Jesus Christ, God revealing himself, and secondly if she is prepared to see in Jesus Christ such a difference of degree of self-revelation as to constitute a difference of kind? If she can go this far, she can postpone action on the virgin birth, the Johannine miracles, and the resurrection.

George Fox once said to a seeker, "Look to that which is good in you to lead you to God." With Evelyn Underhill von Hügel was also prepared to start where she was and to move on from there. "Simply feed your soul on the great positive facts and truths you see already: pray for fidelity to your light, and for as much light as may be within God's plan for you. And as for the rest, neither force adhesion nor allow rejection, but let it alone, as possible food for others and indeed for yourself later on. It does not concern *yourself at present.*"[15]

As for her prayers, he proposed no sudden giving up of her natural theocentric approach. This approach is after all an indispensable movement in the life of prayer. The suggestion rather was to start by asking only for an abandonment of the notion of its exclusiveness and the entertaining at least of the possibility of its being crossed with the incarnational accent. Could she begin by admitting that the theocentric approach is not the way to pray but is rather a way to pray? Could she perhaps pray in her theocentric way to the unincarnate God and then bring into the foreground Nazareth and the Lake of Galilee and Calvary in order to see what the incarnation might have been like and what it cost to "come all the way downstairs?" It is with this kind of gentleness that his guidance was given.

All Custom-Guidance Is Subject to Drastic Modification

The agreement between them was that she was to report to him first of all, each six months, and then in 1923–24, once a year. Her reports are searching and bring his swift response. Once again, his guidance is individual and not by rule of thumb. She has been in a time of desolation! She must scale down drastically the supposed fixed minimum that was to be carefully preserved in consolation *and in desolation* and take up some manual work, which in this case turned out to be a return to the Middle Ages by taking up script writing. She found the need for more than one retreat a year at the Anglican retreat center of Pleshey. She must, of course, have two. Later she feels a need for a longer time of deliberate prayer each day. She must extend the time.

She has had recurrences of her terrible doubts that the whole religious life is only a human projection, is purely subjective. Here von Hügel is firm and sharp with her. "You should see my old man dusting me down," she once said to Lucy Menzies. Can she deny that universality of human need for facing the claimfulness of the surface self on the one hand or the dealing with that need by God and Christ on the other? Do not these facts constitute a snubbing of the loose line that has let her skeptical fancies run free? Or again, she has miscast herself in the wrong ascetical type. She is no Trappist type, no de Rancé. Readiness to abandon her temperamental fancies and inclinations, her overconcern with herself and her failures, to take what God sends to her, to carry on all that she does for God, this is the form of the ascetical call for her.

She feels her unreadiness for intercessory prayer and mentions her wincing before the possible price of such prayer. Graham Greene has said much of this price in his searching play *The Potting Shed* in connection with the priest uncle's intercessory prayer for his nephew's life. "As to intercession," wrote Evelyn Underhill to von Hügel, "if I ask myself whether I could face complete spiritual deprivation for the good of another: e.g., to affect a conversion, I can't do that yet. So I have not got real Christian love: and the question is, can one intercede genuinely for anyone, unless he is ready to pay, if necessary, this price."[16]

Salesian Gentleness in Spiritual Guidance

Once again von Hügel shows a truly Salesian gentleness. She is not to strain after the practice of intercession for others. She is to be very faithful in visits to the poor and in taking the sacraments. She had better go on with her ordinary prayer and in time, perhaps soon, a call to intercession will come. Von Hügel wrote her, "We must always in our own efforts strive to reach what we have not got by the faithful practice of what we have, although God is in no way tied in his dealings with us to this procedure."[17]

Always he tried to draw her quietly away from that inverse form of pride that beats its breast at its own cowardly impotence, its spiritual misery, at its own weakness, and into a consciousness that with the focus on God and Christ and their redemptive action, the self is really transformed. "Develop a general, gradually increasing habit of dropping all voluntary self-absorption during the day and gently turn to God in Christ . . . a gentle, general horror of self and a simple flight away from self to God and Christ—to Christ—God—this will brace you finely." "Drop gently, drop by a quiet burning to God and Christ and the poor, and you will grow in peace and power."[18]

William Russell Maltby once counseled his fellow clergy about their sermons: "One word on sin and nine on the Redeemer," and von Hügel's spiritual counsel carried this same glint. Encourage by directing the mind of the one who prays upon the ultimate source of encouragement. The rest will take care of itself.

Through all of these four years of guidance, there is one further facet that dare not be neglected. For von Hügel, from beginning to end, Evelyn Underhill was a special child of God. She had a special vocation to fulfil. She had a genius that if put to apostolic use might greatly further the kingdom. While he encouraged her to write less, "say two-thirds of your output during the average of the last ten years," and to cut down for a time on her own guidance of souls, it is all with the utter confidence that God will in his good time release her again for her vocation freshly endued with power from on high. Her call to sanctity, to be possessed by the One for whom she was made, must come within the strength and limitation of her body, her mind, her nervous system, her station in life, and this sanctity will come if she will yield to it.

Out of these years of direction that closed only with von Hügel's death in 1925, there emerged a new orientation in Evelyn Underhill's life and writing. She was drawn more deeply than ever before into the life of her own Anglican communion. She wrote to Dom John Chapman, "I owe him (v. H.) my whole spiritual life, and there would have been more of it than there is, if I had been more courageous and stern with myself, and followed his directions more thoroughly."[19]

> Until about five years ago I never had any personal experience of our Lord. I didn't know what it meant. . . . Somehow by his (v. H's) prayers or something, he compelled me to experience Christ. He never said anything more about it—but I knew humanly speaking he did it. It took about four months—it was like watching the sun rise very slowly—and then suddenly one knew what it was.
>
> Now for some months after that I remained predominantly theocentric. But for the next two or three years and especially lately, more and more my whole religious life and experience seemed to center with increasing vividness in our Lord—that sort of quasi-involuntary prayer which springs up of itself at odd moments is now directed to Him.[20]

From this time, her own guidance of souls, her increasing service as a retreat leader at Pleshey into which she poured her best thinking and insights during the last fifteen years of her life, and her books and letters take on a new tone and focus. What she learned for herself from von Hügel's direction, she gave costingly and with a moving abandon to others.

This case study of von Hügel's guidance of Evelyn Underhill does not in any way exhaust the materials at our disposal in studying the Baron's gift in spiritual counsel. The volume of *Letters to a Niece* is available in libraries and this in itself contains a most revealing look into his handling of a young woman on the threshold of life. The correspondence with both George Tyrrell and Maude Petre is also full of this kind of guidance, as are occasional letters to people in every station of life, to say nothing of the rich sprinkling of counsel that is interlarded throughout his philosophical and theological books.

The Pharmaceutical Chest of Spiritual Guidance

What is there to be said in general about the prescriptions of spiritual guidance? What are they meant to do? In one of the Gospel stories, a group of men powerless of themselves to heal a paralytic, were able nevertheless to bear him to the house where Jesus was teaching and to elude the crowd by lowering him from the roof into the presence of the One who was alone able to heal him. All spiritual guidance and devotional practice has for its function only this business of eluding the crowd, of carrying, of bearing, of bringing the persons to be guided more directly into the Healing Presence and then to leave them there. God Himself is the real spiritual director.

There is, however, almost never anything new in this pharmaceutical chest of spiritual guidance. There are no "wonder drugs," no revolutionary surgical instruments, no radioactive applications. Yet the old tested medicines are forever being adapted by a good physician to the special needs of the patient and we can most profitably examine von Hügel as he goes about this work of adaptation.

Of all of these remedies directed at a cure for the inevitable dispersions of life in this world, none is more universally applicable than prayer. "The Christian spirit is a matter of daily self-conquest," von Hügel wrote to Wilfred Ward in 1875, and in that daily matter, von Hügel confessed that he could not get on without the regular use of prayer. Some of this prayer would no doubt be vocal and often in the form of the great classic prayers of mankind. To know that one is not praying alone but is lifted up into a great common tide of prayer is usually a substantial help and very especially in the midst of suffering when single phrases or even words repeated over and over are handholds that one requires. If these bear us into the Presence, that is all that is necessary. But beyond this (although not necessarily above it) is mental prayer and after its obvious phases of repentance and forgiveness, there usually emerges a season of intercession.

Von Hügel says little of the form that his own intercessions took, but he once wrote to his niece,

> I wonder whether you realize a deep, great fact? That souls—all human souls—are deeply interconnected. That we can not only pray for each other, but *suffer* for each other? That these long, trying wakings [his "white nights"], that I was able to offer them to God

and to Christ for my child—that He might ever strengthen, sweeten, steady her in her true, simple, humble love and dependence upon Him? Nothing is more real than this interconnection—this gracious power put by God into the very heart of our infirmities.[21]

Here is the kernel of Charles Williams' insight into what it means to carry one another, the theme about which his novel *Descent into Hell* is written. And here is the reason why intercession may end with no more than Catherine of Genoa's "for these I cannot ask anything from this tender Love: I can but present them in His presence."[22] Yet in other cases, that carrying may bring the bearer as low as St. Christopher's divine burden brought him at mid-stream. Von Hügel clearly had both kinds in mind and the number of friends that he carried in intercession morning, noon, and night was never small.

For von Hügel, the highest dimension in prayer was that of adoration. For here there is no self-concern, no "flea hunting" for sins, no business to transact; only an overwhelming thankfulness that God is what he is and has done what he has done, only the fulfilled "longing aye to dwell within the beauty of His countenance," to know that "we are not He—but He made us," to know that the abyss of his mysterious love is never plumbed, and yet that he gives himself to us forever. It is to be noted that on von Hügel's tombstone in Stratton-on-the-Fosse there is chiseled the psalmist's cry of adoration, "Whom have I in heaven but Thee?"

For those for whom the movements of repentance, forgiveness, intercession, and adoration give way to the involuntary prayer of simple regard, von Hügel has only encouragement. But he gives many hints that the ordinary movements of "deliberate prayer" are still a part of his daily ration. He also suggests that to remember God as we move from one occupation to another throughout the day is good, and that it helps to cultivate that quiet sense of his presence back of all that we do.

Remedial Instruction in Devotional Reading

Again and again in von Hügel's letters there are references to his daily fifteen minutes that he gave to devotional reading. "And I have been so hard worked that, for this kind of reading, I can only find my usual quarter of an hour; which has to go to those few books (*Bible* and *Imitation and Confessions*) which have been my staple food hitherto,"23 or once more, "that daily quarter of an hour for now forty years or more, I am sure has been one of the great sustenances and sources of calm for my life."24 "St. Augustine: I cannot exaggerate the gain that I think you will derive from feeding for years on the *Confession*. They, more than any other book, excepting the Gospels and the Psalms, have taught me and I believe they will teach you."25 "I am so glad you are trying to work the *Imitation* [*of Christ*] into your life: it is the only way to read it which is really worthy of what itself is so intensely alive. Now *there* is a book written as should be all religious books; they should be the quintessence of a long experience and fight in suffering and self-transformation."26

This devotional reading, von Hügel believed, is to be done to lift the sights. It is to reengage the soul in its divine vocation. It is read in the hope that some phrase or line in it may single out the reader's condition, may be an occasion on which God may speak to him, may perhaps convict him of sin or of untilled ground in his life that he has been reserving, or may lure him on in something that may have long since been undertaken but that is lagging.

This kind of reading is there to be distinguished from ordinary reading and his words to his niece about the way to read a devotional book show the seasoned spiritual guide at work once again. Here is a whole set of lessons in remedial reading packed into a single letter.

> Of course such *"reading"* is *hardly reading* in the ordinary sense at all. As well could you call the letting a very slowly dissolving lozenge melt imperceptibly in your mouth, eating. Such reading is, of course, meant as directly as possible to feed the heart, to fortify the will—to put these into contact with God—thus, by the book, to get away from the book, to the realities it suggests. . . . And, above all, perhaps it excludes, by its very object, all criticism, all going off on one's own thoughts as in any way antagonistic to the book's thoughts; and this not by any unreal (and most dangerous) forcing of oneself to swallow, or to "like" what does not attract one's simply humble self, but (on the contrary) by a gentle passing by, by an instinctive ignoring of what does not suit one's soul. This passing by should be without a trace of would-be objective judging; during such reading, we are out simply and solely to feed our own poor

soul, such as it is here and now. What repels or confuses us now may be the food of angels; it may even still become the light to our own poor soul's dimness. We must exclude none of such possibilities; "the infant crying for the light" has nothing to do with more than just humbly finding, and then using the little light that it requires.

I need not say that I would not restrict you to only one quarter of an hour a day. You might find two such helpful. But I would not exceed fifteen minutes *at any one time;* you would sink to ordinary reading if you did.[27]

This most generous of men was always buying and sending off packets of books to his friends and correspondents, and apart from the basic fare already mentioned, the writings of two eighteenth-century French devotional authors were much in favor, Père Caussade's *Self-Abandonment to Divine Providence* and Père Grou's *Manual of Inner Souls.*

There was always a clear distinction between this special devotional reading to be done in its own way, almost in the mood of meditation, and the wide-ranging, voracious, ordinary reading of history, biography, literature, philosophy and science that he was constantly about himself and that in due moderation he commended to others. He was horrified at the rumors that the high Anglican, Pusey, read only religious books. For himself, von Hügel had a bee's lack of fastidiousness in his willingness to gather honey from any available flower. But with all this, specifically devotional reading found its unique and indispensable place in the day's menu.

The Tarnished Mounting and the Jewel

His third prescription to those he guided was that they participate actively in corporate worship. His writings are crammed with ardent testimony to the importance he attached to the corporate aspect of religion. While von Hügel has been popularly known for his championing of the mystical element in religion, a more careful scrutiny of his writings might seriously qualify this impression, and might compel an acknowledgment that his peculiar contribution had tended rather to emphasize the very special necessity of crossing the mystical with the historical and institutional. "Thus mysticism would never be the whole of religion: it would become a dangerous error the very moment it claimed to be the whole; but at the same time it would be an element essential to religion in the long run and upon the whole, although it would, as already said, possess its own dangers, its own besetting sins."[28]

Repeatedly he points out the vocational excesses and extravagances of the mystic, the mystic's bent to individualism, to pantheism, and the rest. Von Hügel's goal seems always to be that of bringing the mystical element back into a creative tension with the historical and institutional, to finding the nail-marked foot of Jesus Christ planted squarely in the door of any such excess and demanding a reckoning, on the part of the mystic, with the historical Jesus and with the institutional conduit of his message to them, namely the Christian Church.

Here in this historical figure of Jesus Christ with which the corporate worship of the Church confronts us, we are back in the company of something greater than ourselves, yet something that as the new Adam, the type man, as the revelation of God, and as the focus of redemptive love, searches and probes our every need and aspiration. Nor is this any local phenomenon. In a famous passage von Hügel insists that in this corporate confrontation, we meet One whom all the ages and races and civilizations will never exhaust.

> For a person came and lived and loved, and did and taught, and died and rose again, and lives on by His Spirit forever within us and amongst us, so unspeakably rich and yet so simple, so sublime and yet so homely, so divinely above us precisely in being so divinely near—that His character and teaching require for an ever fuller yet never complete understanding, the varying study, and different experiments and applications, embodiments and unrollings of all the races and civilizations, of all the individual and corporate, the simultaneous and successive experiences of the human race to the end of time.[29]

The Church, for all of its shortcomings, its failures, its blasphemies, its apostasy (and von Hügel although a Roman Catholic, is the last either to deny or even to conceal them), this hair shirt of some form of institutional religion and of its regular exercises of corporate worship cannot be bypassed but must become a part of the practice of a sin-ridden, short-memoried, flesh-and-blood pilgrim who would let

God have His way with him in this life. For von Hügel, the Church, "at its best and deepest, is just *that*—that interdependence of all the broken and the meek, all the self-oblivion, all the reaching out to God and souls,"[30] and if the skeletal structure of different ecclesiastical organizations offends the angellike vision of many, including his niece, as to what the ideal Church should be like, the old Baron reminds her in his quaint way that "even Cleopatra, when in the splendor of her youth, had such a very useful, very necessary, quite unavoidable skeleton inside her, had she not?"[31]

Deep as is his respect for the spiritual and social witness of the Quakers, von Hügel is never tired of reminding them that they lack a deep enough sense of gratitude for the Bible, for the saints, and for the preservation of the active and regular confrontation by the historical Christ that has come down through history in the Church. For him, this regular confrontation of the worshipper by the historic Christ is an essential, and the Church is the tarnished mounting in which the jewel of Christ is set.

His own view of the Church was naturally closely bound up with sacramental practice. There is something moving in the reports of scholarly companions who occasionally accompanied him on his daily walk on Hampstead Heath. One has spoken of how they were passing the little Catholic chapel on the Heath just as he was making some devastatingly critical remarks on a New Testament text, and of how he hastily excused himself, entered the chapel, sank down on his knees before the sacrament on the altar, and lost himself in prayer. For him there was apparently no incongruity between the free mind and scrupulous adherence to devotional practice. One of his happiest remarks referred to those who were very firm at the center, being able to be quite free at the periphery.

No one in his generation felt more deeply the neglect of the intellectual and scientific element in religion on the part of the Roman Catholic Church or wrote more openly to his friends about the heavy-handed authoritarian pressures that were used to stamp out the modernistic movement in which he played a prominent role. In fact, in 1910, he wrote to Maude Petre of his anticipation of his own excommunication and asked her prayers "and please pray for me that, if and when my trial comes, I may be most carefully, most faithful to my best lights as God may give them to me."[32] Why it did not come has been so frequently discussed as to preclude repetition, but while such an experience unquestionably exercised a restraining hand on any zeal he might have had for encouraging non-Catholics to enter the Roman Catholic Church, it did not modify in the least his profound emphasis upon the necessity of corporate worship and of some historic institutional connection in the nurture and growth of a soul in the Christian faith. Nor did it affect his own passionate love for the Roman Catholic communion.

He had himself lived deeply in fifteenth-century, pre-Council of Trent, Renaissance Catholicism. It was from that age that he had chosen the married laywoman mystic, Catherine of Genoa, to form the focus of his study in the *Mystical Element*. He tells us, too, that he longs to write on Nicholas of Cusa, the great fifteenth-century Catholic philosopher, mystic, and humanist. Perhaps all of this helped develop in him an acute understanding and appreciation of the elements of truth contained in other religious institutions than his own. Yet whether he is speaking to the Anglicans, Evelyn Underhill and Dean Inge, or to the Quaker, Rufus Jones, all three of whom acknowledged their enormous spiritual debt to him, he insisted that no soul is saved alone, and that the personal neglect of the corporate worship of God can only lead to a tragic impoverishment. Such worship can and has helped to rid the soul of an over-isolated individualism and fastidiousness, has helped to elicit from it a great wholesome sense of creatureliness, and has served to bind it to Jesus Christ as a member of a costly redemptive community that dissolves away all barriers.

Corporate Worship and the Achilles' Heel of Psychotherapy

Less to the fore, but no less real, in von Hügel's guidance of souls is the fact that the Church and the practice of corporate worship provides something that keeps the counseling relationship clean. A generation later, the contrast between the inclusion of corporate worship and the situation in ordinary secularized psychotherapy is very striking. For in the close and inevitably dependent relation in which a person stands to the other person guiding him or acting as his therapeutic counselor, certain highly destructive adhesions almost inevitably appear. The significance of these "transference" phenomena has still to be plumbed to its root by psychotherapy, but many therapists find they are so cumbersome and leave such lasting scars, that they have tried all manner of strategems including even the mixing in of group therapy with individual therapy in order to try to rid themselves of this highly vulnerable Achilles' heel or at least to attempt to moderate its effect.

When the one who guides and the one who is guided both require and are regularly engaged in corporate worship, they are swept out of themselves, out of their superior and dependent roles, out of their self-occupation in which all therapy and guidance abounds, and into the presence of One who fulfills and satisfies and not only discloses their need but who renews their courage to live toward him. Here is an objective cleansing that places the whole relationship on a new basis.

At its best there is in all corporate worship an objective, unself-conscious therapy going on that lays hold of any self-conscious therapy that has preceded it, and consummates it. Yet without this act of corporate worship, which always follows the therapeutic processes when these are a part of the normal apparatus of the Christian Church, there is prolonged self-absorption and a network of dependency relationships in therapy that even the most brilliant contributions in the field in recent years have not been able fully to untangle. The regular return to the objectivity of worship, to the confrontation with Jesus Christ, to the self-losing belonging to a redemptive community on the part of both guide and guided, furnished a setting for the therapeutic situation that von Hügel felt to be essential.

On Lightening Ship in Times of Dryness

Evelyn Underhill promptly turned von Hügel's spiritual counsel into a rule of life for herself, and it is true that the practice of preparing such a simple rule of life, of submitting it to the spiritual director, and, after securing his approval, of living by it and then, after a time, revising it in order to make it a more suitable regimen, is a customary formula in spiritual guidance. But von Hügel knew in advance that rough times would come and that even the commitment to a simple rule would tend to be shaken by these inevitable spells of spiritual dryness, these times of inward consolidation, of testing, of what Evelyn Underhill tellingly calls being put on "the night shift." Well in advance, he warns those he guides about these times, and tells them if necessary to lighten ship on their rules until the rough time is over.

> Now what I advise you to do, when spiritual dryness comes markedly into your soul, is to drop all your continuous though mixed prayer—all, that is, except short morning and night prayer; little aspirations during the day, especially acceptances of this dryness; and on Sundays, your Holy Communion . . . ; as soon as without self-probing you see that the dry bout is over, quietly resume your full rule—not till then. . . . Treat your soul as the captains in the old pre-steam days treated their crew. These men had always to be busy, but not always sailing. Weeks of no wind, or of the wrong wind would keep them from sailing. What then! They would at once, as part of their work and life, drop the sailing and take to the mending and making of sails and nets, etc. So do you.[33]

Rules are made for men, not men for rules, and once again the great sanity of von Hügel shines through.

Religious Practice and the Broad Overlap with Common Life

Von Hügel looked upon retreats, that is withdrawing to an appointed house for several days of silence, prayer and religious instruction, as a helpful auspice if they were well conducted and not attended at too frequent intervals. Above all, he does not wish to overtax those he guides, and he fears religiosity like the plague. There were several devices to this end of cauterizing religiosity which he used himself and which he commended to others in the solid guidance that he gave them. He believed that a fairly broad overlap with people in all walks of life helped greatly. He found in the duties and celebrations of his own family an immeasurable boon. He found that his walks in the public gardens daily which brought him close to children and nursemaids were good for him and much prized in his life.

Once more, my Swedish friend Emelia Fogeklou-Norlind had written me of her visit to von Hügel and his family in 1921, eleven years after her first London visit in 1910, when he stood under the pall of impending religious troubles.

> Tall, upright, without any resting-chair, stately with radiant and clear eyes under shaggy brows, he came to meet me looking at least

ten years younger than last time. (I should have liked to see him in Kensington Gardens just beyond with his little Pekinese dog, and a lot of children who without hesitation chose him to tell them the time of day by his watch.) Instead I saw *him* this time as a pater familiae. The merry family lunch at the big round table was unlike the twilight hours in 1910. . . . He was so full of hope, so happy, and also so full of jokes. And when he gave his last greeting at my taking leave, he did not now speak of the duty to suffer and to bear the pain of it, but of the wonderful *Joy to live!* In the copy of Julian of Norwich's *Revelations* which he gave me as a present, he wrote in his big square handwiring, "This shewed our good Lord, to make us glad and merry."

In addition to these ordinary duties heartily performed, von Hügel had a prescription which he had tried on himself and found most bracing. As has been mentioned, he conceived of science and its rigorous discipline of objectivity as a kind of asceticism especially suited to our age, and he counseled anyone who spent much time in religious affairs to master the discipline of at least one science thoroughly. He had been a lifelong student of geology and later had been much involved in textual criticism, and he felt that both of these sciences checked his trying to see things according to his subjective preference and were just the friction that was needed by one in whom the inner life was a primary concern. Furthermore this hard, cold, scientific discipline strengthened the intellectual element and its integrity as one of the elements of the religious life itself.

Heroic Goodness and the Supernatural

Von Hügel's spiritual direction quite naturally aimed at kindling such a fierce love of God that only a life of sanctity would suffice. And sanctity means not only a growing yielding to God but it means suffering and joy, and it means heroic virtue in this world. All around him he found flashes of the supernatural, of another order breaking through into this order in the acts of heroic virtue that tumbled out of ordinary people: a busman, an Irish washerwoman, a territorial soldier, all appeared in face of the wholly unpredictable, uncontrollable, unevadable events that life poured out upon them. For von Hügel, these acts are different from the natural. Thus bodily cleanliness, honesty in buying and selling, submission to the police and due tax-paying to the state . . . all was indeed held to be from God, to be necessary, to be good. But it was only Natural Good. Von Hügel is not against this substratum. But for a Christian, it is not enough. Someone has suggested that if you want to be good, you have got to be heroically good, and von Hügel is pointing to something of the same temper. "A religion is not worth much if it does not produce heroic acts," von Hügel suggests.

> God . . . has put salt in our mouths, and we now thirst for what we have experienced. We now long for Supernatural Good. Supernatural Beatitude. Now acts, acts and dispositions become possible, attractive, even actual within us and by us, which no State, no Guild can ever presuppose or require. Now decency is carried up into devotedness and homeliness and heroism. This is the real and unique work of the Church! "the awakening, the training, the bringing into full life and fruitfulness of the supernatural life."[34]

And this too is the goal of all genuine spiritual direction.

But *"awakening, training, bringing into full life and fruitfulness of the supernatural life,"* clearly this is nothing that a spiritual director can accomplish! This is a task for the Grace of God. For who would dare to claim that he had a formula of basic training for the eruption into being of such heroic life? Or who would dare lay down any rules for what by its very nature is beyond rules, for what astonishes, for what makes us all bow before its authenticity, and yet which must come up from the deep upon an occasion that is anything but deliberate?

Yet even here, von Hügel suggests that some hints are not out of place. One of the universal occasions where this heroism may appear is in the midst of physical and mental suffering in which all men at some time share. Von Hügel gives no suggestion that Christianity has an explanation of suffering. It acknowledges it for the evil thing it is. But while it has no explanation, Jesus Christ, the One who has gone before, has shown the way to transform it and it is this transformation of the unpredictable extremity into an instrument in the service of God which is the indelible mark of heroic virtue, of the emergence of the supernatural.

Holy Suffering Is the Crown of Holy Action

How, then, may a Christian deal with suffering? He, too, may with God's help transform it and make it the thin place in the membrane where the supernatural shows through. One of the things about suffering which von Hügel notes as especially favorable for taking us beyond those things we can manage in our own strength, is that in it we cannot pretend and put on airs. "We cannot, do what we will, cut a decent figure in our own eyes." Rather we are ruthlessly cut down to size. It is in the midst of pain that we have a chance to learn to whom we belong, on whom we can depend, or on whom we may rest our trust when we may be too weak even to lay it there. Here, von Hügel, in some of the most noble teaching to be found in Christian literature on the bearing of pain, teaches us how, when we cannot bear to face it in blocks of a month or a week or a day or an hour, we can face it in terms of this single pain, and the offering up to God of this pain "with the pain well mixed up into the prayer" as a redemptive gift or as an act of intercession for sin, "O may this pang deepen me, may it help to make me real, real—really humble, really loving, really ready to live or die with my soul in Thy hands." "Oh! Oh! This is real: oh! deign to accept it, as a little real atonement for real sin."[35] In 1921 he wrote to his niece of these unexpected occasions of suffering when God gives us concomitant opportunities and graces and growths. "Holy suffering is the very crown of holy action. And God is no pedant. He can and does look to the substance of our suffering and knows how to penetrate beyond our surface restlessness."[36]

He believed that any occasion could be the occasion of the supernatural disclosing itself, and he had a great passion for selecting simple occasions like the very unpleasant one of packing, which his niece resisted, and showing her how this business might be one that could be lifted to God and made the occasion of serving him with joy and gladness. In fact, as von Hügel continues in his guidance, there is almost nothing of the stuff of ordinary life that could not become such an occasion of concomitant Grace, given our deep enough yielding. This is where he brings in his dependence upon the saints for teaching us here on earth that God's joy can be found anywhere, and he notes how the saints serve us by making "goodness attractive" and making the plainest acts sing like Paul and Silas in their prison cell.

Again and again, von Hügel notes that in the canonization of the saint by the Roman Catholic Church, not only heroic virtue, but joy, abandoned, reckless, uncalculating joy, must shine through and be present as an indispensable condition of meeting the requirements.

He sought to live as he taught, and at the close of his life, when he knew he was dying and that he would never be able to finish the Gifford Lectures which he had been dictating and working on up to these days, he said gaily, "I wait for the breath of God, for God's breath. Perhaps he will call me today—tonight. Don't let us be niggardly towards God. He is never a niggard towards us.—Let us try to be generous and accept. . . . I would like to finish my book—but if not, I shall live it out in the Beyond."[37]

His final words to his niece whose young life he had sought to awaken to the call of God beyond the ordinary line of duty, are words that seem fitting to close a treatment of his role as a spiritual director:

> Our great hope is in Christianity—our only hope. Christ recreates. Christianity has taught us to care. Caring is the greatest thing— caring matters most. My faith is not enough—it comes and goes. I have it about some things and not about others. So we make up and supplement each other. We give and others give to us. Keep your life, a life of prayer, dearie. . . . Keep it like that: it's the only thing, and remember, no joy without suffering—no patience without trial —no humility without humiliation—no life without death.[38]

Notes

1. From a copy of the original letter supplied by Emelia Fogelklou Norlind.
2. *Selected Letters of Friedrich von Hügel,* ed. by Bernard Holland (London: Dent, 1927), p. 266.
3. *Eternal Life* (Edinburgh: T. & T. Clark, 1912), pp. 374–376.
4. *Sermons on Canticles of Canticles,* 69:8.
5. Gwendolyn Greene, *Letters to a Niece* (London: Dent, 1928).XXV.
6. *Essays and Addresses* (Second Series) (London: Dent, 1926), p. 232.
7. Gwendolyn Green, *Letters to a Niece* (London: Dent, 1928), p. xxix.
8. Margaret Cropper, *Evelyn Underhill* (New York: Harper, 1958), p. 70.
9. Gwendolyn Greene, *Two Witnesses* (London: Dent, 1930), p. 101.
10. Gwendolyn Greene, *Letters to a Niece* (London: Dent, 1928), p. x.

11. Margaret Cropper, *Evelyn Underhill* (New York: Harper), p. 69.
12. Ibid., p. 71.
13. Ibid.
14. Ibid., p. 75.
15. Ibid., p. 96.
16. Ibid., p. 107.
17. Ibid., p. 95.
18. Ibid., pp. 111 and 124.
19. Ibid., p. 68.
20. Ibid., p. 98.
21. *Selected Letters* (London: Dent, 1927), p. 269.
22. *The Mystical Element of Religion* (London: Dent, 1908), Vol. II, p. 127.
23. *Selected Letters* (London: Dent, 1927), p. 203.
24. Ibid.
25. Ibid.
26. Ibid.
27. Ibid., p. 229.
28. *The Reality of God* (London: Dent, 1931), p. 91.
29. *The Mystical Element of Religion* (London: Dent, 1908), Vol. I, p. 26.
30. *Selected Letters* (London: Dent, 1927), pp. 269–270.
31. Ibid., p. 270.
32. Ibid., p. 185.
33. Margaret Cropper, *Evelyn Underhill* (New York: Harper, 1958), p. 97.
34. *Essays and Addresses on the Philosophy of Religion* (London: Dent, 1921), 1st series, p. 283.
35. *Selected Letters* (London: Dent, 1927), p. 231.
36. Ibid., p. 390.
37. Gwendolyn Greene, *Letters to a Niece* (London: Dent, 1928), p. xlii.
38. Ibid., p. xliii.

PART TWO

In Solitude

*Bethlehem Revisited**

It is good from year to year to revisit Bethlehem and to reconsider its miracle. Bethlehem does not change, but *we* change, and the eyes with which we are able to see change. Hence what we see from year to year is not the same, which makes this annual visit an adventure rather than a routine pilgrimage.

If we were to be literal about the visit, we should find present-day Bethlehem a small town of some 6,000 inhabitants a bare five miles south of Jerusalem. It has an elevation of some 2,500 feet, as Jerusalem has, but instead of being set on a hill, as my wife from her caroling acquaintance with Bethlehem was led to expect, it lies in a valley. In its streets flocks of sheep and goats swirl about motor cars and slow them to a creeping pace, and Western-dressed Arabs mingle with those of flowing gowns and turbans.

The spot where Jesus was born was probably in a grotto or cave on the edge of old Bethlehem, or so at least Justin Martyr in 150 A.D. described it, but this is today overlaid by a vast church and a cluster of religious houses. What is believed to be the actual spot where Jesus was born is in a bejewelled crypt around which hang perpetually lighted lamps: six Greek Orthodox, five Armenian Christian, and four Latin or Roman Catholic, with mass being celebrated here daily by the Greek Orthodox and Armenian priests. Pope Paul VI's visit to Bethlehem a decade and a half ago was to try to make these lamps shed a more kindly light to each other and hence outwardly toward the world.

If we are trying to reconstruct the original scene in the cave, we

* First published as Pendle Hill Pamphlet 144 © 1965 by Pendle Hill, Quaker Study Center at Wallingford, Pennsylvania 19086. Used with permission.

must wipe away this ceremonial splendor and see the work animals, oxen and donkeys, tethered in their stalls. Tended by her faithful husband and lying on the straw, a young woman has just given birth to her first child. The child has been wrapped in swaddling clothes and laid in a manger.

Francis of Assisi could make all of this more vivid to us than the bejewelled crypt, for he had the custom on Christmas Eve of reenacting this scene in an Italian barn, and for him the placing of the child in the company of animals and straw of the fields was so naturally right. Francis had passed through the needle's eye of God's mercy and his fear had been taken from him: fear of nature, fear of animals, fear of men, fear of death. He knew that we were meant to live at peace with each other. The saints who have literally lived with wild animals that terrify most men have done it because of this fearlessness that comes from baptism into the peaceable kingdom. For Francis no jewels or lamps or mosaics were so expressive as the return to the primitive scene, where straw and animals were grouped together with a holy couple whose child was to disclose this cosmic peace and love to the world. And so it was that Francis preached his Christmas sermon from the floor of a barn.

Selma Lagerlof, the Swedish novelist, once wrote a little volume that she called *Christ Legends* and for me the most beautiful of these is called "The Wise Men's Well." I shall not relate it all, but one scene in it may bring us to a Bethlehem that is even nearer than that of Francis's manger scene: the three Wise Men, drawn by their common vision of a rapturously beautiful star that bids them seek a newborn King, follow this star across desert and plain until it stands over a grotto in Bethlehem. But when they look into the grotto they see only a young peasant woman and her husband with a newborn child. They turn away in disappointment, to find after they have gone some distance that they have lost the star and with it the memory of where they have been. Then, overwhelmed with a sense of guilt, they know that they have allowed their earthly judgment to lead them astray. In their shattering remorse they come upon an old well, known to the inhabitants for its mirroring qualities. They sink down in despair at its side until one of them, wishing to quench his thirst, suddenly finds in the depths of the well the reflected image of the lost star, and looking up to the sky, discovers it there. Thus they are led back to the grotto where they pay their homage to the hidden king.

This legend of the Wise Men's Well has recalled to me the words of the seventeenth-century Angelus Silesius who declares:

> Were Christ a thousand times reborn in Bethlehem's stall
> And not in thee, thou still art lost beyond recall.

For the well in which that wise man found the star was surely the inner Bethlehem of his own heart. In our times of solitude this well is open to each of us, and its power to mirror in its depths the cosmic significance of what took place in Bethlehem is always there, always open. Pascal in his *Thoughts* says that all of the troubles of the world come from the fact that a man cannot remain in his own chamber. What does he mean? I think that he means exactly what Selma Lagerlof's Wise Men discovered: that when in stubborn self-will you refuse direction and lose the star of rapture, you can recover your direction only by looking into the inward well of your own heart. Only as you return to your chamber—the chamber that lies open to each of us if we dare to stop and enter into it—will you be restored to that which you most deeply long to find: One who can take away all fear; One who can restore you to living on the earth, sowing your life as a seed in those about you; One who can take away the haunting fear of death by using your life in His and your fellow man's service.

Let us look into the Wise Men's Well we carry always about with us. Let us enter into Pascal's *Chamber* and see what this inner Bethlehem is like and what this wonderful seed, Jesus, that was sown in the heart of the world, really means to our lives. I often ponder about how, if there is a God who cares for what happens to human beings on this or any planet, and if he was consumed with love and knew that only by love could men and animals and his world of nature live peaceably together, and he wanted to communicate, to disclose, to unveil this to them most effectively, how he would do it. I once played a game where we put on a charade and hoped to communicate what we were trying to say so effectively that our partner, who had been out of the room when we made it up, would guess what it was we wanted to say and express it. I remember how hard I tried to give him the clue and how I longed for him to grasp it, and how long he fumbled before he understood.

I cannot see the life of Jesus as other than God trying to disclose his love for us and his attempt, at any price, to show us that the cosmos is grounded in love. All hate, all sin, all discord, all clefts, all ignorance, all confusion will finally give way to love. But this love, like a strip of wood, has its grain that must be followed. If we follow this grain we will find that we must change the patterns in which we have previously cast our lives. And I do not see how God could have made this disclosure more effectively than by placing his love in the body of a child who was to become a man, and letting this cosmic message shine through the material envelope of a human life.

There is a Zoroastrian legend, according to Professor Zaehner, that the pre-existent souls of men were given the free choice between remaining forever unharmed in eternity or of going down to earth *"to do battle with the Lie."* But the Incarnation, while accepting that Jesus came freely and chose freely all through his earthly life, never identifies the *battle with the Lie* with the destruction of the stream of matter into which he entered. Archbishop William Temple was right: Christianity is the most materialistic religion that ever existed. For William Law was speaking accurately of Jesus when he said that "Till the day of his death, his *process* seems to have been natural." When he walked, he needed rest; when he was hungry, he ate; when he was tired, he slept; when he was dispersed, he went into the mountain or a desert place to be collected. In none of this is there a contempt for matter. Rather, we see a man who draws matter together as he turns Godward at each moment of decision. He does what the Jews call "hallowing" matter, drawing it as a precious substratum into its true role. And as such he is a man. He is indeed the Son of Man—for this is what man is called to do.

What a heritage this leaves to the Christian religion as one that has no fear of matter in a world where God the creator and sustainer is working in matter! The actual Lie with which battle is to be done is always two-fold: on the one hand, the repudiation of matter and the specious attempt to purify spirit from all touch with it—on the other, the attempt to make matter and its patterning all that there is, to deny that it can be hallowed and to claim that back of its mysterious swirls there is nothing which is its source and ground.

The struggle that Hinduism and Buddhism are having with the technological revolution and with the physical sciences of our day, to which they find it so terribly difficult to adapt, comes from their denial of any genuine reality to matter and their focus on purifying themselves from any trace of it. The West and all of us within its pattern of cultural expectation are little tempted by this form of *the Lie*. The Lie with which *we* must do battle is the opposite temptation to assume that matter and its patterns which science has ferreted out *are all that there is* and that our humanity is a passing shadow and has no ultimate significance, or that our prowess in discovering the scientific laws of matter will ultimately be capable of fathoming the laws of human conduct and will enable us to condition men and women to interact as society in its Brave New World may wish them.

Jesus not only worked within the natural process but he respected it; he drew his images from it, his parables from it. He sawed and planed and shaped wood in a shop. He fed the multitude and his disciples when they were hungry, and he used a net to catch fish and a boat to cross the lake. But always in his healing he reached through the context of the laws that control matter to their living ground and allowed these very laws by extending them, just as psychosomatic medicine has hallowed medicine, not repudiated it, by showing how the patient's faith, his life *Anschauung* affects the way his body responds to surgical and chemical treatment. I have a friend in New York, a great eye surgeon, who has kept careful records on several hundred cases, and they seem to him to establish the fact that in his operations, the life view of the patient affects the amount of anesthesia that it is necessary to use in order to put him under, and affects the rate of healing of the tissues after surgery. The Christian religion has only encouragement for science and the laws of matter which science discloses. It knows that with every step science takes forward, the universe reveals itself as being governed by the same laws that govern human thinking. This is exactly what would be expected of the world that Jesus depicted where matter and its laws have a legitimate and significant status. But Christianity also knows that there is revealed in Jesus a faith in a mysterious ground to these laws that is continually expanding them and drawing them into a deeper harmony.

If I want to run a sewer or a water line across the beautiful garden spot beside the Haverford College Library which we all love and cherish as the heart of the campus, what I need is a contour map of that piece of ground. No amount of love for the spot can be any substitute for the rather grim and curious abbreviation of the area which the contour map with its spindly concentric lines represents. But if I want to appeal to your son to come to Haverford and to show him what a beautiful campus we have, a watercolor painting of that garden is far superior to showing him a contour map. If I were a Druid worshipper and wanted you to grasp what that wooded garden was really like in spiritual significance, a religious dance might communicate it to you more adequately than either of the other two. Yet no one of these depictions of our library garden either exhausts its meaning or repudiates the others, although the Lie, with which Jesus does battle, insists that it must.

The great Cambridge astronomer, Sir Arthur Eddington, once told a story in order to indicate the different worlds in which all of us live and operate, and to lay the ghost of the claim that the causal world of science is the only world that exists. Speaking in England, he referred to the Armistice Day observance of the eleventh of November when in Britain everyone stops for three minutes between 11:00 and 11:03 A.M. and silently remembers the sacrifice of the departed and the cause for which they gave their lives.

If a team of scientists from Mars should arrive in Britain on such a day, prepared to observe with accuracy exactly what took place in those three minutes, they would find men and women exerting energy to throw their bodies out of the irregular movement known as walking, and coming to a halt. They would find motorists applying foot pressure on brake pedals, and bands in brake cylinders tightening against drums with sufficient friction to bring the cars to a standstill. They would find ignition keys turned off, and engines ceasing to function. If they entered factories they would observe men throwing switches to cut off the power that operated rows of machines. At exactly three minutes after eleven they would note the reverse action: men and women throwing their bodies out of equilibrium and beginning to walk; brakes released and ignition circuits restored; starters applied and cars moving again; the switch in the factory thrown, setting motors, shafts, machines in motion.

These scientists might now return to Mars with a perfect causal account of all the activity on that particular section of the earth during those three minutes of time, without having the slightest notion of what was really taking place in those silent moments of remembrance.

Professor Eddington did not tell this incident to discredit causal law or to discredit science—a field to whic he had devoted his life. He was only suggesting that important as causal law may be, it does not exhaust the situation. It might even turn out that all causality was an aspect of a deeper teleology. The radical differences between these worlds of discourse, Professor Eddington believed, should compel us to continue our search for their inner connection. The witness of Jesus was that spirit and matter are friends, not enemies. And if we pursue this we should not be surprised to find that matter and body through the long evolutionary process have been host to consciousness and awareness, and that awareness has been host to love.

This is what Teilhard de Chardin has been saying with great effectiveness when he talks of *convergence*. It is almost precisely what I have referred to as the hallowing of matter, with the child of Bethlehem revealing the cosmic goal of love. All of a piece with this is Jesus' insistence that life be used to the full: that each person's talents be used and not buried; that death is not all; that we may all participate in this process of luring the cosmos toward love.

As we sit at the Wise Men's Well, pondering what it means to have Jesus born in our own inner Bethlehem, that Son of Man discloses to us a further insight into the human species. It is that the love and salvation to which Jesus draws all men is not solitary but is solidarity. He is come to draw all men into the way of love, and he is the center of a community of all men. Charles Peguy in his beautiful poem, *The Mystery of the Charity of Joan of Arc,* says, "We must be saved together, we must come to God together. Together we must be presented before Him. Together we must all return to the Father's house." Here he seems to be saying exactly what Jesus was suggesting. If there is a loving One at the ground of things, then this explains the infinite caring and concern for the *outsider* that marked Jesus throughout his swift life: his concern for the harlot, the prisoner, the lunatic, the leper, the blind, the Quisling tax-gatherer, the Roman Captain, the Samaritan. What is Jesus in his concern for them saying but this, "I am the cornerstone which the builder rejected of a building that shall house all." His smashing the parochialism of the Judaistic community, which felt so secure in its private covenant with God, was all a part of this. God can raise out of the stones men who are more faithful than Israel. His command to share the good news of the God of love with all of the world means that there are no more limitations. His ethic is the same. It is unlimited liability for all men, and there is no relaxing this to our own ethnic or national group or to some regional Atlantic community. Here is a universalism of caring that breaks every last bond.

During Vatican Council II, I have witnessed the transformation of the Roman Catholic Church under the leadership of Pope John XXIII and Pope Paul VI. It has come out of its solitary castle where it had maintained a defensive siege mentality since the Council of Trent. Now it joins the world with a passionate concern to heal the former separation by Brotherhood in Christ. There have always been exceptions, always those who have refused to acknowledge those walls of separation, and I recall Harry Emerson Fosdick's telling incident of a priest in the first World War who was giving spiritual help to a dying Protestant boy when the lad said, "But Padre I don't belong to your church," to which the priest replied, "But you belong to my God." In John XXIII's vision, which the Vatican Council II at its best was trying to implement, this spirit is no longer the exception but is a sustained attempt to reach beyond all boundaries.

In the Second Session of the Vatican Council, Cardinal Suenens told a story of a visit which John XXIII made to a Roman prison one day. Pope John was the despair of his security forces for on almost no notice at all he was always going out into his diocese of Rome to pay visits, and on this particular day he said that he was going to see some of his good children in prison since they were not free to come to see him. Pope John preached to them in the prison on the mercy and grace of God that could forgive any sin, and after the sermon he came down among the men and a murderer stepped up to him and asked, "Your Holiness, does what you said about the mercy and grace of God hold, even for me?" John did not reply. He simply put his arms around the man.

This is the kind of inclusiveness that is revealed in John's reaching out beyond the confines of the Roman Catholic Church to both Christians and non-Christians. Nor did he stop even here, but longed to witness to those in no religious group whatever, those who belong to what Paul Tillich calls the Latent Church, as against the Patent Church, which is made up of all who, through their service to others, reveal that they know something beyond themselves. What John wanted the Roman Catholic Church to realize is that Jesus brought the news that Love was at the ground of the universe to all men. He reminded his church that the infinite yearning love of God, and of the whole community of the living and the dead who care, is drawing at the hearts of all, and that Roman Catholicism will be the prisoner of its own religion if it does not proclaim this broader message both in word and deed. Even the lines of the sacred and profane melted before Jesus' blazing vision, and it is fascinating to hear a famous Dutch Catholic theologian insisting that God is at work in the secular world and that the church can never find His full message of salvation unless she buries herself in that world. It was fascinating, too, to hear the former Swiss Ambassador to India, Jacques Cuttat, a Roman Catholic, declaring that only as Christianity engages in the most open and receptive dialogue with Hinduism and its profound treasures of meditation and simplicity of life will it find what the Holy Spirit has to teach it through such an encounter.

All of this is a witness to Jesus' message that he came to draw *all* men, and that no religion can ever be exclusively concerned about either individual or denominational salvation but only about the lifting of all men into a community of interdependence. I had an old Swedish friend who late in her life wrote a book about the luminous center that she believed characterized our boundary-destroying age. The person and the message of Jesus, which has broken every known boundary of race or nation or wealth or natural gift, draws us toward this luminous center that knows no boundaries.

I once received a Christmas note from some Carmelite Catholic friends of mine who have struggled desperately to maintain a little center for contemplation on the outskirts of Sedona in Arizona and who have made incredible sacrifices to establish another such center in Nova Scotia, an hour's ride north of Yarmouth. Their Christmas prayer seemed to me to be directed not to me alone but to us all. "May the fierce love of Jesus drive out of us all vapid and shallow peace. With wild joy and a plea for prayers, Yours, Father William."

As we return to Bethlehem and look in solitude into the Wise Men's Well of our own hearts, we know with Teresa of Avila that "This is not the time to rest." We are called to go on our way at such a season with Jan Ruysbroeck's wonderful words ringing in our ears. Speaking of Jesus, he said, "All that he was and all that he had, he gave; and all that we are and all that we have, he takes."

SIX

Solitude and Prayer

It may be of interest to know how an essay of this sort came to be written. In 1965, inspired by the strong ecumenical thrust of the Second Vatican Council, a group of some twenty persons chosen from Roman Catholic and non-Catholic scholars and writers in the field of Christian spirituality gathered as the guests of St. John's Abbey in Collegeville, Minnesota, for a week of close fellowship and sharing. Out of this gathering grew a modest Ecumenical Institute of Spirituality that since that time has met each year for three or four days nearly always in a different setting in order to experience something of the varying flavors of the different Catholic orders and of the Protestant and Orthodox spiritual centers that housed us.

At one of these meetings, two papers were presented on Loneliness and Solitude. One dealt with a psychological and sociological analysis of contemporary Western man and of his loneliness as one of the spoiled offspring of our so-called affluent society. The other paper, written out of a decade of intimate experience in nursing homes, gave special insight into the bone-deep loneliness of many of the elderly in our contemporary scene. In the course of discussion, we felt the need to have a further look into the very nature of human solitude itself and to see what light this condition of solitariness might throw on our relationship to God. When asked to prepare such an essay on Solitude and Prayer, I found that I had never before singled out this aspect of solitude and was intrigued and challenged by it. Hence what follows.

Only a few months before his death in 1971, Damasus Winzen, Abbot of Mt. Saviour, and a beloved member of the Ecumenical Institute of Spirituality from its beginning, told one of his Benedictine brothers in the monastery, "When I look back upon the seventy years of my own life, I see quite clearly that I owe my present inner happiness, my peace, my confidence and my joy essentially to one fact: I am certain that I am infinitely loved by God." This precious confidence that he shared at the close of his rich but often painful life gathers up, witnesses to, and exposes what to me is the very ground and goal of Christian prayer. For at the existential base of each person's nature there is a homing trend. Man longs for cosmic confirmation. We all know Augustine's formulation of this longing, "Thou hast made us for thyself, and our heart is restless until it rests in Thee."

Harry Williams, an Anglican member of the Community of the Resurrection, wrote so extravagantly about Alan Ecclestone's *Yes to God* being the best book on prayer to be written in this century that I managed recently to get a copy of it in England. I felt warmed when I found Ecclestone saying again, "Prayer remains the means by which we grope our way towards that which alone can satisfy the profoundest need of our human life: to know that we are known and loved by God" (p. 7). George MacDonald a century ago counseled Christians to "Pray to the God of sparrows, rabbits and men, who never lets anyone out of his ken." Christian prayer is many things and has many facets, but undergirding them all is the longing for the restoration of the awareness of the presence of the love that "never lets anyone out of his ken." Von Hügel sums up the setting of this restoration of awareness in a single line, "It is God who awakes, and it is God who slakes our thirst."

If our thirst for cosmic confirmation and caring is secretly longing to be quenched, and if God's transforming love yearns to quench that thirst, what are the conditions under which this double search of human beings for God, and God for human beings, can best be carried out? Prayer is obviously a proven channel. But prayer that transforms seems to require certain optimum conditions that tilt us towards its authentic practice and that clear the way in spite of the dispersion and the web upon web of preoccupations which tend to usurp our earthly life. When I go in to have my chest x-rayed each year, I am required to strip off my ordinary bodily coverings and to expose my chest to the piercing rays of this light. Solitude, solitariness, seems to express a similar preparatory readying function in its stripping me and preparing me for exposure to the radiant beams of love that the x-ray focus of prayer accomplishes.

A naked definition of solitariness would point simply to aloneness; absence of involvement in company. When Alfred North Whitehead in the most frequently quoted line in his *Religion in the Making* says that "Religion is what a man does with his solitariness," it is clear that he means more than aloneness. For when solitariness moves into a religious dimension, a man is not only physically apart but he has begun to ponder who he is and why he is as he is and what his life is meant for. Whitehead also seems to be implying that solitariness is the right climate for this further dimension. He wraps up the matter with his blunt: "If you are never solitary, you are never religious."

Francis Bacon, an earlier philosopher, treats solitariness itself less admiringly than does Whitehead when he says, "Whoever is delighted with solitude is either a wild beast or a God." But even Bacon hints or dimly senses a spiritual element in solitude. For Whitehead, its religious dimension depends upon its use: "What a man *does* with his solitariness." One can *do* more than one thing with this sense of my separateness, my aloneness. It can lead me into despair, into melancholia, into life-flight, even to suicide. In my efforts to shake it off it can lead me into all kinds of specious attempts to hide in the crowd and try to bury myself in the crowd's bestial rhythms. We seldom in our time have people trampled to death in a rush to enter our churches or our monasteries. There seems to be at work in our contemporary culture almost a demonic passion to avoid solitude and to merge with a crowd. But genuine solitude can also nurture fierce honesty about ourselves and lead us into the deepest interior discoveries when it is linked with prayer. Again, linked with prayer, it can become an almost indispensable dimension in the matter of discernment of the spirits and in winnowing out the leadings and concerns and decisions that come to those who pray.

People have long puzzled over what Jesus meant by suggesting withdrawal into a closet to pray. Was this simply to cleanse their prayer of a possible lurking self-display of piety if it were done publicly? Or is this closet a synonym for solitariness, for aloneness?

In Tokyo, William Johnston took my wife and me to visit the Jesuit residence that is within easy reach of the students in several universities. A large room was set aside for meditation, its walls empty except for a single scroll that hung from the center of the wall which the students faced when they came over in sizable numbers to meditate.

He translated for us the verse of Scripture, Hosea 2:14, that was written in Japanese characters on the scroll. It read, "I will entice you into the desert and there I will speak to you in the depths of your heart." The verse links solitariness with prayer in an almost inimitable way. For until I have been lured into the desert, until I have then been brought in solitude to the very ground of my being, where I am beyond the grip of my surface self with all of its plans and distractions, I am not able to hear the divine whisper. Fénelon has a telling line, "How few there are who are still enough to hear God speak." In genuine solitude this stillness returns. Jesus' counsel, then, to take to the closet when we pray links prayer and solitude and is both blunt and penetrating. Nhat Hanh, the Vietnam Buddhist sage, repeats it in his own words, "Before you can meditate you have to learn to close the door." Regarding meditation as I do, as a way of withdrawing from the world with its outer and inner barrage of distractions and of opening the way for prayer, I look with the deepest gratitude on this preliminary stage of solitude that is involved in "learning to close the door."

Interestingly enough, this solitariness, this desert stillness where God may speak to us in the depths of our hearts, is not only a principal requirement of prayer but also of genuine creation in nearly every area. Ralph Harper writes, "We know that serious things have to be done in silence. In silence men love, pray, listen, compose, paint, write, think, and suffer" (*The Sleeping Beauty*, p. 111).

There is a lovely description of a Chinese painter, Wang Li, that depicts him in the elusive creation of one of his paintings. The inner brooding of the painter in this time of gestation makes of him a solitary in all else that he does while the inner vision matures and he is inwardly cleansed and prepared for the final movement of "I have it." Here is what Wang Li says:

> Until I knew the shape of the Hua Mountain how could I paint a picture of it? But even after I had visited it and drawn it from nature, the "idea" was still immature. Consequently I brooded upon it in the quiet of my house, on my walks abroad, in bed and at meals, at concerts, in intervals of conversation and literary composition. One day when I was resting, I heard drums and flutes passing the door. I leapt up and cried, "Now I have it." Then I tore up my

sketches and painted it again. This time my only guide was the Hua Mountain itself.

Writing itself, like other forms of creation, can be a form of solitude as anyone knows who has worked with a subject until the "I have it" moment comes. Thomas Merton says, "Writing can be an occasion of prayer and contemplation. Writing is the one thing that gives me access to some real silence and solitude" (quoted in James Forest, *Thomas Merton,* p. 39). This access to silence, to solitude, that writing requires, points to a kind of emptying: a slipping out of the grip of our world's fierce clutch of artificial respiration and letting normal breathing take over once more. Solitude is a way of restoring in us an interior space that is meant to be there. It not only liberates a writer, it opens the way for the soul's answer to the Love that enfolds it—the answer of *Yes to God.*

We can learn a good deal from our children. Frances Wickes, a leading Jungian therapist for a long generation, tells of a seven-year-old child brought to her because of his sleeplessness. The child confided to her that he had to wake up at night to think "because you can't think in the day. There isn't time." His mother had filled his days with so many opportunities.

Most children, when they have not been bedeviled by our galloping extrovert culture with its heavily programmed day-care centers, its elaborate nursery school curricula and its TV programs that have been designed to fill every hour of their day, actually have the root of this longing for patches of agendaless solitude within them. Our older daughter saw to it when she was about five or six that she had what she called her "secret place"—a little wooden chair that was well hidden inside a forsythia bush in our yard. She made it clear that this place was "off limits" for others and she loved to repair to it and to know it was there even when she was about other things.

My wife recalls that she occasionally had a guilty conscience about having been away so often when our younger daughter came home from school. Years later this younger daughter let her read an autobiography that she had written in an English class at the boarding school she was attending. In it was the younger daughter's account of remembering how wonderful it was after a day in school to come home to an empty house and to be able to be alone and quiet! The taste for solitude is not only an adult discovery.

I have spoken not only of the important role of solitude in taking us into the heart of prayer but also of the way it furnishes the climate for creation in almost every field. I have also mentioned the strong root of it inherent in children that have managed to survive the fierce extrovert passion of our culture. In the practice of interior prayer, as in the entry into worship, it is fascinating to observe how different religious bodies have learned to enter it by some act that breaks with ordinary life: a Jew dons his prayer shawl; a Muslim unrolls his prayer rug; a Roman Catholic reaches for his rosary. By these acts each is distancing himself from his usual preoccupations and seeking an apartness, a solitariness, even though he does this in the company of others.

A seventeenth-century Quaker, Alexander Parker, underlines this breaking act of solitude for Friends entering their place of meeting in preparation for abandoning themselves to a waiting form of interior prayer. "The first that enters into the place of your meeting, be not careless, nor wander up and down either in body or mind, but innocently sit down in some place and turn in thy mind to the light, and wait upon God simply, as if none were present but the Lord, and here thou art strong. Then the next that come in, let them in simplicity of heart sit down and turn in to the same light, and wait in the Spirit, and so all the rest coming in in the fear of the Lord sit down in pure stillness and silence of all flesh, and wait in the light. A few that are thus gathered by the arm of the Lord into the unity of the Spirit, this is a sweet and precious meeting in which all are met with the Lord. . . . Those who are brought to a pure, still waiting on God in the spirit are come nearer to the Lord than words are . . . though not a word be spoken to the hearing of the ear. In such a meeting where the presence and power of God is felt, there will be an unwillingness to part asunder, being ready to say in yourselves, it is good to be here, and this is the end of all words and writings, to bring people to the eternal living word." (*Letters, etc. of Early Friends,* ed. A. R. Barclay, 1841, pp. 365–566).

It is important to note that the singling out of the solitary individual can take place in corporate worship as well as in private prayer and if it is deep enough, the promise of the line from Hosea may be fulfilled. In a corporate Quaker meeting for worship I have often experienced times of being taken into the desert, into solitariness, and from time to time of being spoken to in the depths of my heart. All of the inward stilling meditational exercises, whether of Hindu Yoga or Muslim Sufism or Zen sitting or the *Cloud of Unknowing's* centering meditation that Basil Pennington has helped our generation to learn, are themselves little more than means of moving toward the desert where we may in rare moments experience the further enticement and the being spoken to in the depth of our hearts. Yet to move toward the desert where interior prayer and interior transformation can take place means a willingness to go into the desert, to learn to shut the door, and to move into the necessary solitude which prayer and the deeper levels of worship require.

I do not want to focus upon the frequently quoted psychological and sociological accounts of loneliness and solitariness which are involuntarily imposed on so many in contemporary society. But it would be wrong to neglect some of the most striking of these involuntary situations. If looked at carefully, they may be able to give us insights into the redeeming possibilities that lie hidden in solitariness even when life has seemed to impose it completely without the person's consent. So often involuntary, unwilled solitariness, after a season of kicking and screaming, turns out to be a genuine enticement into the desert where we are spoken to in the depths of our hearts and from it we may emerge as released souls. Katherine Mansfield speaks of how "Everything in life that is accepted undergoes a change."

There is the solitariness of an aged person whose friends have nearly all slipped away into the beyond; the solitude of a sick or injured person who has been lifted out of the stream of active life; and the solitude of our waking hours in a sleepless night, what von Hügel called his "white nights." Martin Buber confided to a friend of mine his being asked a whole procession of grandiose-sounding questions by an audience one night until finally he burst out with "Why don't we ask each other the questions that come to us at three o'clock in the morning as we lie tossing on our beds?" Thoreau says somewhere that we can learn more about ourselves in a sleepless night than by a trip to Europe!

I need not go on enumerating these situations where unwilled solitude has, when properly used, led to the reenactment of God's promise in the verse from Hosea. Life's "nutcracker" is what Fritz Kunkel called these chapters of involuntary solitariness. Fritz Kunkel was himself a liberated man, "psychotherapized," as he used to put it, by the loss of his right arm in World War I and so promoted from surgeon to psychotherapist. He saw these lonely separated-out situations of solitariness as precious openings, as gifts of another chance. But he knew that they were effective gifts only if they were accepted and acted upon.

At Wainwright House in one of our retreats Dorothy Steere met an architect who was paralyzed from his waist down and in a wheelchair. He told her of his bout with polio in mid-career, and of having a wife and five children to support. To be sure he had, wheelchair and all, struggled his way back into his profession and had succeeded, but he went on to add, "You know, Mrs. Steere, the tragedy of my situation is that with all this suffering, I haven't learned a thing from it." Like a flash of lightning, coming to a man lost in the woods, solitariness that comes from life's nutcracker may suddenly show him where he is and give him a glimpse of the real path ahead to be taken. But the man himself must be willing to trust the flash and walk the path it opened to him.

One of the most profound experiences of involuntary solitariness that we all face as mortal men and women is the prospect of our own death. There is a story of Philip Neri, the late sixteenth-century founder of the Oratorian Order, who was a much beloved listener to the irrepressible ambitions of the young men who came to his oratory in Rome to speak to him. One day a charming law student was telling of how he already had earned a degree in civil law and now was studying canon law. "What then?" Philip Neri, the listener, asked quietly. "Why then I shall be called to the bar and practice law." "What then?" murmured Philip. "Why then I shall marry and inherit a large estate from my family and raise a fine family of children." "What then?" asked Philip. "Why then I shall make a great career in the law and may even be elected an Orator of the Rota." "What then?" asked Philip once more. "Why then I suppose I shall die like everybody else." "And what then?" asked Philip, putting the penultimate question. The facing, not of death, but of *my* death is one of the experiences of involuntary solitariness that searches a person to the very bone marrow.

Pascal points out in his shrewd way that all animal-kind die, but that, as far as we know, only human beings know that they are going to die and live with this knowledge always present. This marks us out not only as unique, but also as recipients of an invitation to solitude that might almost be compared to a Zen Buddhist *koan*. Such a koan, as you know, is given to a Zen Buddhist postulant to gnaw on until it finally shatters his complacent surface mind and is capable of releasing a whole new layer of consciousness, a *satori* experience that is marked by humility and creatureliness and compassion.

Soren Kierkegaard, as a Christian existentialist, dedicates his powerful devotional classic *Purity of Heart* to "That Solitary Individual." In it he does his best to cut man off from refusing to face the prospect of his own death in the course of his flight from God. Kierkegaard believed that only as man came to the end of himself and recovered a condition of solitariness, of being taken into the desert, could he be brought into the transforming presence of God, who alone could both individuate and tender him. Kierkegaard strikes at man's attempt to escape solitude and to hide from God by plunging into the *crowd*. The *crowd* for him is the opposite of solitariness. If, throughout his life, a person has succeeded in depending upon soft companionship, abundant advice, the group, the crowd, Peer Gynt's "middle way," and has managed always to succeed in insulating himself from solitude by being constantly in the company of others, Kierkegaard points out that in death, at least, he will be confronted by what it means to be a "solitary individual." At this frontier the path narrows and all must travel Indian file. Death isolates, and before the prospects of death all props are withdrawn; all leaves cancelled; all makeup is removed and one's individual being is brought into view. The whole of *Purity of Heart* is lighted up by the image of a person alone before the Creator.

From some references in the *Journal,* I suspect that Kierkegaard imagined the situation of death to be something like the exposure of a person on Soren Kierkegaard's beloved Jutland Heath in which the sparsity of all vegetation left no place where one could possibly run or dodge or crouch or lie prone and not still be exposed to an observer's view. In the words of the old Black spiritual "There'll be no hidin' place up there." He describes this singling-out process which death involves, the process of isolation that dissolves away the crowd, that shuts out the many voices that have enabled him until then to wheedle and compare, and that leaves his own conscience alone before the Eternal. Here is a koan-like paragraph in Kierkegaard's own words:

> In eternity, conscience is the only voice that is heard. It must be heard by the individual. . . . It must be heard. There is no place to flee from it. For in the infinite there is no place; the individual looks about for the crowd. Alas, it is as if there were a world between him and the nearest individual, whose conscience is also speaking to him about what *he* as an indivudual has spoken, and done, and thought of good and of evil. . . . Eternity never counts.
> . . . In eternity you will look in vain for the crowd. You will listen in vain to see whether you cannot hear where the noise and gathering is, so that you may run to it. In eternity you, too, will be forsaken by the crowd. . . . For in eternity crowds simply do not exist.
> . . . Yes, here in the temporal order it is possible that no individual can ever succeed . . . in dispersing the crowd . . . the crowd shouts mockingly at God, "Yes, now see whether you can get hold of us;" yet, since it is difficult in the rush of the crowd to distinguish the individual . . . the sober countenance of eternity quietly waits.
> . . . Eternity scatters the crowd by giving each an infinite weight, by making him heavy—as an individual" (*Purity of Heart,* Harper Torchbook 1956, 186–193).

In the prospect of death a spiritual gravitation is revealed. Each is indeed made heavy as an individual. Lines here and there from Psalm 139 might furnish a kind of refrain to Kierkegaard's severe text: "Thou hast searched me and known me. . . . Whither shall I go from thy spirit or whither shall I flee from they presence? . . . The darkness and the light are both alike to thee. . . . Search me, Oh God, and know my heart, Try me and know my thoughts."

This stripping in Kierkegaard's and the Psalmist's confrontation of our ultimate situation pierces very deeply into the role of solitariness in the life of prayer. Kierkegaard's repetitive note that in our finitude and our mortality we can't run away from God, we can't run away far enough, throws much light upon why we feel secretly threatened by solitude and by prayer. For both solitude and prayer are occasions when we *are* ultimately made still enough to hear God speak. It seems plausible that our lapses in prayer and our endless ingenuity in the ways of avoiding solitude are both clearly connected with our fear of the regrouping of our resources that will occur if we come into God's presence. For to come near to God is to change.

During World War II, a Quaker artist friend of ours who lived in East Berlin painted a water color of three men standing some distance away but in clear view of Christ on the cross. Each man was holding his mask in his hands and looking up at the crucified one with a mingled gaze of longing and fear: of longing to follow the way to which the Christ beckoned him, and of fear both at the loss of his mask which the sight of Christ on the cross had struck from him and at the price that following the new way might exact of him.

A husband once confessed, "The one thing I can't stand about marriage is the honesty about myself it crams down my throat." Marriage and solitariness, strangely enough, have the same propensity in this matter of self-revelation. But the unmasking that both involve can be a preparatory threshold for the humbling, the tendering and the flood of compassion that true love between two persons effects and the bottomless gratitude and love for God which authentic solitude and prayer releases.

Dr. William Sullivan, a spiritual leader of a generation ago, expresses with impressive insight the debt he owed to his early Roman Catholic seminary training in the use of solitude:

> There is no species of training that I ever underwent to which I owe more than to the habit of regular periods of inner solitude. Solitary we must be in life's great hours of moral decision; solitary in pain and sorrow; solitary in old age and going forth to death. Fortunate the person who has learned what to do in solitude and brought himself to see what companionship he may discover in it. What fortitude, what content. By a great blessing I had an aptitude for these hours of quiet reflection and grew to love them. . . . To be alone and still and thoughtful bestowed upon me the richest joy I knew and for this priceless cultivation I shall be thankful always.

In recent times there has been some inclination among New Testament scholars to translate the line in the Lord's prayer "Lead us not into temptation" to read "Do not put us to the test." We cannot fully understand solitariness without going a step further in examining its role in actually putting the solitary one to the test. It is hard to see either Jesus' or Paul's experience in the wilderness, after each of their callings, as other than a test. Three centuries later, the desert fathers found in their solitude in the desert an unleashing of almost irresistible temptations. They report that they were swept by a consciousness of the powers of evil, of abysmal depths of pride, of lostness, of infidelity and of unsurrendered areas in their own lives. In solitariness they became aware all afresh of the deprivations, the misery, the injustice and callousness of the hurtling world that they had fled but that, in spite of their apartness, they still carried within them. Yearning as they did for this world's redemption that was hidden in their hearts, the powers of darkness were forever tempting them to despair of it as lost.

Georges Bernanos, in his powerful study of sanctity in the novel *The Star of Satan,* depicts this pushing open of the floodgates of evil that any life being powerfully drawn toward sanctity seems to be vulnerable to. When George Fox, early in his account of his adult spiritual life, was brought to experience "an ocean of darkness," this was no passing whimsy. That he was brought to see that this "ocean of darkness" was "overcome by an ocean of light" made no less searing and shattering what had preceded it.

John Woolman (1720–1772) was perhaps as near a saint as any Quaker has ever managed to come. He tells us in his very honest *Journal* of a journey he undertook late in his life, together with a companion, in order to return a visit that a group of friendly Indians had made to the Quakers in Philadelphia. On the journey they had to pass through hostile Indian territory and night after night their very lives were on the block. One night as his companion slept soundly beside him on the ground, John Woolman lay awake until almost morning, unable to sleep and riven with evil thoughts and inward self-accusations. He felt that perhaps he was willfully continuing this dangerous journey and risking his companion's life as well as his own, not because God had called him to this journey but out of fear of being ridiculed at home as chicken-hearted if he now turned back! He adds that "the gracious Father who saw the conflict of my soul was pleased to give quietness," and then he adds that he "got a little sleep towards day." The test.

Thomas Kelly tells of an experience when he was on his knees in Cologne Cathedral at the close of a long summer of visiting suffering German people in Hitler's grim repression in 1938. He speaks of how he felt the weight and pain of evil pressing him almost unbearably down into the very stones on the floor on which he was kneeling. Finally he was relieved by a presence that bore the weight with him. Again, the test.

Returning to Jesus and the powers of darkness that he faced in solitude, questions of Jesus' own sanity that so greatly troubled his family that at one point they sought to take him out of circulation could hardly have been prevented in his solitude from rising like mists in his own mind to query his mission. The tightening coils of the great serpent that threatened to destroy father and sons in the Greek caring of the Laocoön do not come far from depicting Jesus' times of solitude as in the temptation scene when he recognized and agonized over the diabolical projection upon him of the popular expectations of a con-ventional power-wielding Messiah—a Messiah who would use force to drive out the foreign power of occupation, exalt Israel over its neighbors, and confer upon Israel a tidal wave of worldly prosperity! Again in the Gethsemane scene where options of evading those who were about to destroy him were still open, and where the noose of God drew ever tighter, the presence of the powers of evil is evidenced by the agony of his decision even though total abandonment to God's will was finally sustained. Once more, the test.

Friedrich von Hügel is impressive in pointing out that as far as Jesus was concerned, the Gospels give us no hint of Jesus belittling the power of evil in the tests. Nor is there any attempt there to join those Greek philosophers who seek to explain evil away. Instead, von Hügel insists, Jesus' approach to evil was to take it into himself and transform it and to promise us that we, too, through the Holy Spirit, might be given power even to surpass him in that transformation.

The times of doubt, of spiritual dryness, of the dark night of the soul that few veterans of the life of prayer ever escape, are often so acute that the cry "Do not put me to the test" of the Lord's prayer is a human, all-too-human, response. But in these seasons of solitariness, Job's "Though he slay me, yet will I trust him," if adhered to, seldom fails to reveal that in reality a deep consolation has been taking place and that under the cover of this season of darkness the person has been brought to a new level of clearness. A wise spiritual director in such situations gives "a paw in the dark" as needed, but is careful not to intrude in the costly interior process of reshaping that is going on.

In my hope in this essay to get an actual picture of the power of the dimension of solitariness, I wrote to Jane Richardson, a nun of Loretto who has lived quietly as a hermitess within half a mile of the Mother House at Nerinx, Kentucky. I have visited her more than once, and in a letter I put several questions to her about what fruits the solitariness of these years had brought to her, what they had cost, and where the peaks and pitfalls of such a life of voluntary solitude lay. Her beautifully simple reply in a way almost rebuked my queries. I felt a little like the inquirer who asked Dögen, the father of the Soto school of Japanese Zen Buddhism, on his return in 1227 from spending many years in China with great Zen masters, what he had learned in all of this time he had been away. Dögen replied, "O nothing much, just softness of heart!" I want to share a part of this letter, to say a word about solitude and solidarity, and to conclude.

Jane Richardson writes:

> Briefly, nine years of living in quiet escape a certain kind of scrutiny simply because they are, in being solitary, quite ordinary and uneventful, so to speak. The burdens and fruits, in other words, seem to resemble those of so many not living in solitude—at least, as I hear my friends and visitors. Of course, the style is different, the flavor of the learning and dying and rising—of the struggle to believe in love and to ever choose life—has its own uniqueness. If anything, I am more aware than ever before how similar *all* our lives are, inasmuch as the universal call that persistently draws our hearts onwards has its origin and end in the one same Goodness, the one same Spirit, the one same Mercy and Compassion. Solitude for me has meant a way of learning that, of coming to a knowledge of what I used to believe: that we all share the Great Life of God, that we can, in your own words, "touch the thresholds of the lives of others in the Being of God where we are all interrelated." The poets are right: no one is a stranger, a foreigner. For those who live, latitude and longitude, fences and rivers, literacy and bankbooks cannot determine kinship. Nor for sin . . . it is clear that Mercy holds us all, and will find a way to lead us into glory, even though we enter "kicking and screaming," as Auden says somewhere.
>
> Besides this fundamental sense of human communion, solitude has also meant for me simplicity. Nothing (very) dramatic has happened—no outstanding successes or failures (no exciting play-offs!), nothing worthy of special attention, yet everyday living prov-

ing sufficiently satisfying to my sometimes restless, sometimes stilled human heart. I search now for honesty so as neither to overvalue or undervalue a style of life that has so become mine as to be almost impossible for me to objectify or evaluate. I'm sure it is true of solitary living as of community living: each person translates it uniquely. So "solitaries" are not of a mold. Yet there are common features, of course—such as the emphasis on listening, the expanding of the interior landscape, both in the direction of exposing painful weakness (others and self) and in the direction of compounded hope and knowing awareness. . . .

Its fruits? A sense of rightness about my life. Increasing hope of life for everyone. Great communion with sisters and brothers everywhere, of all times, past, present and future. Joy that never stays away for long. New skills that I like: chopping wood, modest carpentry, writing music for the Word that nourishes and sustains me. A poor spirit at peace.

In this frank sharing of her life of voluntary solitariness, there are many fine insights. But the one I want to have you especially note is that in her almost total apartness, she finds herself brought ever closer in love to the persons and the world she has left. Thomas Merton, a few years before his death when he was already living as a hermit, was taken into Louisville for some medical treatment. The car arrived at an hour when the workers were pouring through the streets and as he looked out at them through the window, he was overwhelmed with a feeling of love and oneness with them and he felt every vestige of spiritual superiority or human differentiation being wiped away. He knew now that they were one, and he longed to leap out and embrace them.

In both Jane Richardson and Thomas Merton it is intensely revealing how their solitariness merged with interior Christian prayer led them to a new dimension of solidarity. This solidarity is not based on pity for the victim or a hate of the oppressor. It springs from a response to overwhelming love. When John Woolman writes in his *Journal,* "My heart was tender and often contrite, and universal love for my fellow creatures increased in me," he was witnessing to that solidarity that dissolves away all walls and opens the pores of the world so that it can breathe again.

This discovery of solidarity that Thomas Merton and Jane Richardson have made through an extended period of solitariness makes no claim to be more than one way in the service of God. The monastic fallacy that regards its pattern as *the* way or even the *highest way* is not likely to be the temptation of our time. In the end, the ground of solidarity as the ground of interior prayer is one and the same. It is to discover at the heart of things that our solitariness is transcended and that we are not alone but that *He* is in this whole scene with us, and that we are all in this together.

How wonderfully gathered up all of this is in a letter of counsel thought to have been written by the anonymous writer of *The Cloud of Unknowing* that says,

> Silence is not God, nor speaking; fasting is not God, nor feasting; solitude is not God, nor company. . . . He lies hidden between them and no work of yours can possibly discover him save only your heart's love. Reason cannot fully know him for he cannot be thought, possessed or discovered by the mind. But loved he may be and chosen by the artless, affectionate longing of your heart. Choose him, then, and you will find that your speech is become silent, your silence eloquent, your fasting a feast, your feasting a fast, and so on. Choose God in love. . . . For this blind thrust, this keen shaft of longing love will never miss the mark, God himself. (*A Letter About How to Read One's Interior Inspirations, in Contemplative Review* 10(1977) 15–16.)

SEVEN

Contemplation
and Leisure*

I have never been able to understand how there could be any sound treatment of leisure without a thorough familiarity with at least the lower levels of contemplation. For if we are not to linger in the social and economic aspects of the problem of leisure and are drawn to move on into the human and interior levels, the matter of discerning where, if at all, leisure leaves off and contemplation begins is instantly before us. I shall try to approach the nature of contemplation in a fashion that will, while not wholly neglecting its highest spiritual and philosophical aspects, nevertheless focus upon contemplation's basic root in human beings. In carrying out such an approach, I hope that useful light may be thrown upon the massive congruity that exists between leisure and contemplation.

In the matter of contemplation I shall try in a variety of very plain ways to make clear that contemplation is not meant to be the possession of a gifted or a favored few, but that it is a potential dimension in all human experience and that until this dimension is in some fashion present, the experience is likely to be thin indeed.

You may well ask me at the outset what I mean by contemplation. There are times when an oblique answer may be better than a direct one. I once talked for half an hour with an old Zen abbot in Kyoto and finally I pressed him to tell me whether the new times, which he had been complaining about, called for new koans (the insoluble problems that are given to the monks in order to help them to weary

* First published as Pendle Hill Pamphlet 199 © 1975 by Pendle Hill, Quaker Study Center at Wallingford, Pennsylvania 19086. Used with permission.

out the surface mind and to bring the deeper mind into play). He replied to me by saying, "Please come out into the garden and see my roses!" Obliqueness has its virtues. There is a story in Thomas Traherne's *Centuries of Meditations* which says:

> It is storied of that Prince (Pyrrhus, King of Epire) that having a conceived purpose to invade Italy, he sent for Cineas, a philosopher and the King's friend, to whom he communicated his design and desired his counsel. Cineas asked him to what purpose he invaded Italy. He said, "To conquer it." "And what will you do when you have conquered it?" "Go into France," said the King, "and conquer that." "And what will you do when you have conquered France?" "Conquer Germany." "And what then?" said the philosopher. "Conquer Spain." "I perceive," said Cineas, "that you would conquer the whole world." "What will you do when you have conquered all?" "Why then," said the King, "we will return and enjoy ourselves at quiet in our own land." "So you may now," said the philosopher, "without all this ado."[1]

Curiously enough, each of us has a philosopher, a contemplator if you like, within us. It is a gift that is not optional but that is built-in equipment. This inward companion of ours is able to carry on quite as ruthless a querying of our actions as Cineas managed for the King of Epire. As a matter of fact, this kind of inner dialogue may be going on in us all the time if we are only aware of it. It keeps on asking us, "What, in this world, are you doing?" "Who are you?" "Where did you come from?" "Where are you going?" "Is this foreground of your life, in which you live such an agitated existence, all that there is?" "Have you taken your companions, your wife, your children for granted?" "Does each of them have a destiny of their own and do you know how you are really related to them?"—And a thousand other queries. I once shared in a small colloquium with some Zen Buddhist and Christian scholars in Oiso, Japan, where each spoke very frankly about how he had been moving in his own inward journey. We were startled at the emotion that at times broke through as a Japanese Christian scholar spoke of the Buddhist layer that was always at work in him. In the expression of this emotion, we realized that this Buddhist-Christian dialogue, that may have come into the open for the first time, had long been going on in the deeper reaches of his being, but it had been largely ignored until this very startling moment. There is a strange power buried deep in a man that enables him to carry on an inward dialogue between layers of his own being. It sorts over the raw experiences that come to him and permits him, if he gives it a chance, to stand aside, to look over his own shoulder, and to scan his life plans. It goads him to relate to his consciousness the mysterious wraith of mystery and wonder that hovers over them all. This power in human beings is the rudimentary stub of what might be called contemplation.

When Viktor Frankl in his system of logotherapy suggests that the fundamental drive that is to be found in man is not for sex, or for power, but is the drive for *meaning,* he seems to be feeling after this same ground in us that I have been describing in terms of this inner dialogue—this stub of contemplation. We, too, might find some help in defining contemplation if we put it in terms of a sustained scrutiny for meaning. If we use the metaphor of the eye, contemplation could be described as the power to look steadily, continuously, calmly, attentively, and searchingly at something. Thomas Aquinas para-phrases this nicely in calling contemplation, "A simple, unimpeded and penetrating gaze on truth."[2]

I have called this the stub of contemplation, and I would like to develop that expression because many people tend to identify contem-plation with its most exalted forms, and lose the flavor of it as it may appear as an undertone or dimension of the whole of life. The French Quaker writer, the late Marius Grout, who won the Goncourt prize for his contribution to literature in 1943, once wrote, "I believe in the influence of silent and radiant men and I say to myself that such men are rare. They nevertheless give savor to the world . . . nothing will be lost so long as such men continue to exist."[3] I believe with Thomas Aquinas that "It is necessary for the perfection of the human society that there should be men who devote their lives to contemplation" (*Commentary on Proverbs*), and would express my deep thanks for the contemplative orders like the Carthusians and the Carmelites and the Cistercians, who cultivate this life and who seek to live it out in a sense for us all. But I want at the outset to have us see that the concluding words of Marius Grout are quite as important when, after his tribute to what the special men and women of radiant life do for us all, he adds, "If there is a wish we should wish today, it is that we might see in ourselves the beginning of such contemplation."[4]

When a woman hangs a picture over the sink where she washes the dishes three times a day and when she lifts her eyes to that picture and is not taken away from the job that is before her but lifts the job up into the vision that that picture gives her, that experience springs from the same stub of contemplation. When a man sits on the porch after a hard day's work and, with or without the haze of tobacco, thinks over the day with both its knocks and its beckonings, that is a shoot that comes from the same root of contemplation. When a child comes home from school and goes out into the meadow behind her house and lies on her back and smells all the smells and hears all the sounds and sees all the turning of the clouds, that is contemplation. When a man looks with awe and wonder at a sunset and is swept by the swiftness of life and a sense of thankfulness for the day just passed and for the assurance of the day that will come when this trusted companion of the skies will rise again, that is contemplation—quite as definitely contemplation as when in 1953, at the turn of the New Year, Dag Hammarskjöld, recording his own contemplation, could write: "For all that has been—thanks! To all that shall be—Yes!"[5] Now this may seem a far cry from the speculative contemplation of the professional philosopher or the mystical contemplation of the religious saint. And you may cry out that this is surely all on the natural level and cheapens and blurs for you the whole notion of contemplation. Let me blur it a little further then. I want to go on to suggest that contemplation needs to be seen as not necessarily requiring a separate act or a separate place or a separated situation of time in which it will be performed.

I once knew a mother who gave her son twenty minutes of love each day and singled out the child for that purpose. Now there is nothing to be sneered at in a third of an hour of anyone's tender loving care, least of all of a mother's. But the thing that is incongruous to us and that makes us snort at such a regime is that there is on our part an assumption that this tender loving care is standard equipment on the part of a mother in relation to her son. If this standard is too high, there is still a revolt in us that it should be so contrived and so self-consciously doled out at a given time in a given place. There would be far less uneasiness about the matter if each time the son appeared or when the mother's time permitted it, she turned to him with a loving attitude. This comes very close to what I want to say about the common use of contemplation. It can take place anywhere, at any time, in any circumstance, and its naturalness is the neglected factor.

I tried one time to learn to fashion small knitted squares called "weave-its." I was told that I could occupy my hands in my many committee meetings and that the effect on me would be therapeutic. To my disgust, I found that I was like the old Mississippi steamboat that had such limited steam power that the captain had to stop the boat each time he wanted to blow the whistle. I had either to give my whole sense to the "weave-it," or to concentrate on the committee meeting proceedings, but I was clearly incapable of doing both at once. You may well have the same objection to the suggestion that has been made here that these acts of genuine contemplation can be carried on as a dimension of other activities. But do not lose sight of the fact that I was a novice in this business of knitting in meetings, and that there are those who know what it is to "work collectedly" and to have this capacity for glancing at the frame of meaning in the very midst of their daily work or their family involvement.

William Blake is not writing for the recluse when he says, "There is a moment in each day that Satan cannot find." And Natalie Victor, a hard-driven mother, is not writing for the cloister when she says, "Twenty-four hours to do the one thing needful, instead of ten or twelve to do a dozen. There will be time to place ourselves at the disposal of anyone in real need; no time to waste at the street corner. There will be time to play with the children, no time to be devising schemes for our own amusement. There will be time to read widely, deeply, generously, no time to waste on trivialities. . . . There will be time to pray long and passionately for the coming of the kingdom, no time to doubt its present security or its ultimate triumph."[6]

In an unpublished paper, Mark Gibbard, a British Anglican monk, goes as far as to interpret contemplation in terms of hearing and of attentive listening, and to find in this perceptive listening to his fellows an exercise of contemplation. He believes that any form of behavior *can* be contemplative.

At the Goethe Festival at Aspen, Colorado, in 1949, when Albert Schweitzer and William Ernest Hocking and Ortega y Gasset were present, Ortega y Gasset is said to have crossed to the great auditorium immediately after breakfast one morning and as he entered, a woman stepped up to him and said, "Is this Mr. Ortega?" The Spanish existentialist philosopher gazed at her, paused for a moment, and then replied, "No, Madam. Just a poor inadequate representation of the *authentic* Ortega." That look, to take in her question, and that sharing of a flash of his own inner dialogue, was a flash of contemplation. Sometimes it is not an unexpected meeting with a woman at a door, but life itself that asks me a question in the form of an accident, or an illness, or a sudden change in circumstances, or an utterly undeserved piece of largess. These can be passed off as readily as Ortega y Gasset could have passed off the query of this woman. Or they could be looked at, paused before with an open mind in order to find out what was to be my inward answer to the real question that life was asking of me in that event.

At Harvard, Professor Whitehead used to speak about this possible inward dimension to all experience as "an offensive against the repetitive mechanism of the universe," and I hardly know how we could better characterize one of the aspects of contemplation than this. Perhaps when this repetitive mechanism is resisted in a relationship with another person there is also a kernel of the deepest charity, for then each situation is new, fresh, demanding, and the one who is listening, listens in a fresh and open way.

What I want to emphasize before going on is that the worst disservice we could do would be to commit the heresy of identifying this act of contemplation with a block of empty time or with the provision of an empty space, or to limit it to a certain peculiarly endowed class of persons or, in Greek fashion, to a social class that was drenched with leisure. Contemplation is, as we have insisted, standard equipment, and can never be completely identified with vacant spaces in life or with freedom from responsibility.

I like the earthiness of John Cowper Powys's words about contemplation taking place not on the edge of life but in the very thick of it: "All the nobler instincts of our race are born in solitude and suckled by silence. This solitude need be no far away wilderness in Nature; this silence need be no Himalayan peak. You stop for a second as you cross your city square and glance at the belt of Orion." I know what Powys means by those words because for many years I myself had a strip of open meadow that I often walked at night between my Haverford College office and my home, and on a clear night there was an utterly unobstructed view of the stars. To lift the eyes to those stars was to be searched. George Tyrrell used to say of a fusty, self-ridden colleague of his, "He does not look at the stars enough." And a clergyman whom I know tries at least once a year to preach a sermon on astronomy in order to bring his congregation into this experience. Powys continues:

> You lie awake for a while as you rest in your bed and listen to the storm; and behold! from a few simple elements belonging to that mystery which you have been brought up to call "Matter," there comes over you this reversion, this conversion, this transmutation of spirit. Thinking of your mood later, you will say to yourself: "I felt that while I was listening to the rain." Or you will say to yourself: "I felt that while I was out in the wind." Or you will say to your friend, "It was that walk at dusk when I got as far as the river that made me change my mind!"[7]

Now after all that has been said in the way of domesticating contemplation and bringing it into the common life of us all, there would seem to me to be no basic contradiction in confessing frankly that if this discovery of contemplation, which we have seen as so precious an element in our common life and relationships, should ever become of central concern for our society, ways would almost certainly be found for devising special places and special times and special attention for its direct nurture and cultivation. But as we turn to what our own Western society's priorities may be in these troubled times, and to what this special nurture might consist of, let us never forget what the greatest contemplatives have always maintained, namely, that it can be practiced anywhere and that it is open to all. E. I. Watkin, an English lay philosopher of great depth says, "Only the man who sees nothing beyond his nose, who lives in routine and unintelligent obedience, or who drifts aimlessly through life, cannot or will not contemplate."[8] Evelyn Underhill, in referring to what Augustine Baker calls "all conditions capable," insists that "ordinary contemplation is open to all men; without it they are not wholly conscious or alive."[9] She goes on to connect, without any radical discontinuity, this common openness with the highest glimpses of ultimate togetherness which the mystic witnesses to when she says, "The spring of the amazing energy which enables the great mystic to rise to freedom and dominate his world is extant in all of us, an integral part of our humanity."[10] In no other way can we account for the extraordinary resonance that such mystical personalities have for men and women of the most varied stations and types.

As for our Western type of society in the present scene and the place it gives to contemplation, you do not have to burrow into empirical evidences with the intensity of a Pitirim Sorokin to brand us as a "sensate society" that has seemed to abandon its gift for reflection. I sat with my eyes closed in a back pew of the great cathedral nave in Cologne several years ago and was absorbed in silent meditation. Suddenly I felt a sharp stroke on my shoulder and looked up to find one of the uniformed beadles of the cathedral standing over me and accusing me of using the cathedral as a place to sleep. This was, to be sure, in West Germany and not the United States. And I was in a Roman Catholic cathedral where traditional practice uses kneeling for the exercise of mental prayer. But the experience seemed to me not unsymbolic of our time. If I was not posturally doing something, I was asleep, and this was no hotel, and I must either wake up or get out! There are signs along our superhighways that say "No Stopping Except For Repairs," and they mean it. (In driving on the Los Angeles freeway some years ago, I was forced into the truck lane by a police car because I was only driving 55 miles an hour!)

Architectural styles swiftly reflect the life of the people that they are fashioned for and are therefore a solidified exhibit of the life of almost any period. The disappearance of the porch on our houses is something to think over. This old porch represented a contemplative element in American life and was a place to spend leisure, a place to sit and think and look out on the stream of life. But it has now been found to be expendable, and the first thing that an architect customarily does in revamping an older house is to remove it. Lewis Mumford, in his classic on the culture of cities, notes that in the modern house there is no room that is built for meditation, prayer, or reflection. The medieval house would never have dreamed of being without such a room. Today the house has no inwardness; it is all thrown out toward nature. The bathroom is the only place in the building where one can be sure of not being intruded upon! In Sweden, where glass bricks and glass partitions were used thirty years ago as separations for offices, I was told that one man brought a pail of paint and painted his glass walls so that he could have at least a skim of privacy in his daily work operations. These are but a few of the architectural mirrors of our inward condition.

If we look at such a practice as travel, it has been noted that no people in the history of the world has ever been as widely travelled as Americans are today, but that in no people has it made as little difference to their outlook. We have heaped experiences on top of each other with such profusion that we have never got around to inquiring what they mean for us. Something like the same thing has come through the revolution in communication that has in my own lifetime increased the psychological population, that is, the number of people I am aware of through the printed page, through pictures, radio and television, by hundreds of times. Yet there is in some ways less inner feel of responsibility for those in distant places or near at hand than there was a century ago. This profusion of awareness has not increased man's stature or deepened his inward well of compassion. Instead it has diminished the personal man, the interior man, and has led him forever to be demanding some more novel form of dispersion. The ebb of compassion and the jostling of images in the breast of modern man produces a kind of inner numbness, an incapacity for deep feeling, and the poet's words about being "cut off outside ourselves," or being "distracted from distraction by distraction" are all too well known to us. The Communist world today is protected from this condition in much of its area only by its shortage of consumer goods.

The situation might be summed up in the word "vulgarity" if there were not in it a more tragic element than that word would indicate. For where there is a lessening of humanity and compassion, there is a shrinkage in the capacity for imagination, for walking in the moccasins of the other, and this is a time in the world's history when we dare not run short in such a gift or we mark out mankind for extinction.

I have spoken principally about the West, but it is moving to have Professor Hisamatsu, perhaps the greatest interpreter of Zen Buddhism in Japan, tell a little group of Zen and Christian scholars, in a message that he sent to them, what he saw their task to be: "All we human beings are now threatened by the crisis of the split of subjectivity, its confusion and its loss. To reverse this crisis and to create a stable postmodern original subjectivity—this is the universal and vital task." In a similar colloquium in India between Hindu and Christian scholars, a remarkable Roman Catholic scholar, Klaus Klostermaier, expressed the West's stake in the bank of inward awareness which the common Hindu people of village India still possess. He told this group, "I think that Indians should know that the highly secularized West has a deep appreciation for the amount of spiritual life that is still present in the common people of India. If this spiritual substance in India in the hearts of the common people should be lost by influences in India today which tend to depreciate it and rub it out, the whole world would be the loser. We must help each other, we Christians and we Hindus, to preserve this precious tradition in India."

There are many dimensions to this "spiritual substance in India" that Klaus Klostermaier speaks of with such reverence. I have personally been searched to the core in the matter of the climate of true leisure and contemplation by the Indian attitude toward time and toward the whole matter of flowing my life along planned channels that I have chosen for it.

My wife and I first visited India almost thirty years ago and entered it through its Eastern gate: the city of Calcutta. Some months before our arrival, I had written to William Cousins, our American Friends Service Committee representative there, asking him if he could arrange a time when he might visit the great Indian painter, Jamine Roy. Early in the afternoon of the second or third day of our visit, William Cousins, who was married to an Indian woman and was deeply rooted in India, came in an old taxi to take us to the painter's home. As we got into the taxi I asked him what time we were due at Jamine Roy's house. He casually assured me that we had plenty of time. When we had settled in on our journey, I repeated my question and he smiled and said that the painter was so looking forward to our visit. A half hour further on, I made my query more specific and asked him the exact time we were expected to arrive. William Cousins, whom I had known in America, shook his head and laughed at me with a kind of gentle, charitable patience and explained that Jamine Roy had been expecting us for a month; that he had seen him recently; that he was always at home; and that whenever we got there, he would be ever so glad to see us. He added with a chuckle, "Douglas, you are not in Philadelphia, you are in India. But you are still running on Philadelphia time!"

When we finally arrived, William Cousins was right. Jamine Roy was there. He was wonderfully welcoming. He spent the rest of the afternoon with us. And before we left, he begged us to return again as soon as possible. It began to dawn on me that in India the flow of time and the inward events that it contains is less lashed to a plan than we are accustomed to in the West.

A week later we travelled up to Bolpur and stayed at the guesthouse of Tagore's old center, which has now become the University of Santiniketan. In preparation for the visit, I had asked an Indian professor friend in Calcutta to suggest a philosopher whom I might try to meet while at Santiniketan. He brushed aside the suggestion and said that on his scale none of the professional university philosophy professors there could begin to be as interesting to me as a remarkable pundit or unattached scholar who lived in the town of Bolpur itself. He promised to write at once to an old Gandhian friend of his who was a Bolpur rice farmer and a member of the Bengali legislature, and who, he felt sure, would be happy to introduce me personally to the pundit.

The morning after our arrival at the guesthouse, we were finishing an early breakfast there, when I noticed a boy of perhaps twelve standing behind me and waiting. I asked him what he wished and he told me that his father (the Gandhian farmer-legislator) was waiting in Bolpur to introduce me to the pundit and that he had come over on his bicycle to fetch me. I thanked him, but explained that I had no idea when his father would get in touch with me and that I had already made several appointments for this very morning and could not possibly come with him. I added that perhaps I could come tomorrow or the day after. He simply repeated that his father was waiting for me in the town of Bolpur to take me to the pundit. After I had again explained why I could not come, he repeated this a third time! I dissolved. Messages were sent to each of the persons I had arranged to see that morning with apologies and a request for their suggesting another time. I hired a bicycle-rickshaw and followed the boy on his bicycle into the town of Bolpur.

There I met his father. The father took me to the pundit's house and made the necessary introductions. The pundit fortunately spoke

English and so I thanked father and son and said that I knew they had many duties and I would not presume further on their kindness or their time. The father looked at me with surprise and said he would not dream of leaving; that he and his son wanted ever so much to be in on the visit. So we settled down on our little mats on the floor of the pundit's house at about eight in the morning and the fascinating visit with this inwardly glowing pundit went on for four full hours. Heavily sweetened tea and plates of Indian delicacies made their mysterious appearance from time to time, slipped in noiselessly by his wife, who was never really seen nor introduced.

I finally looked at my watch and saw to my astonishment that it was past noon. I said I must leave at once to join my wife for our appointed lunch at the guesthouse. The pundit objected strenuously. "You cannot possibly leave now," he insisted, "we have only just begun. You must stay on with us for at least a month. My wife will look after you and care for your needs!" I expressed my thanks for the wonderful morning's conversation and withdrew. But as I jogged back to Santiniketan in another bicycle-rickshaw, I began to realize that Philadelphia time and Philadelphia planning were strangely irrelevant in this Asian setting. In India the "spiritual substance" of an inward view of time and of a life flowed through its silent channel is more than a myth.

Vivekananda, the great disciple of Ramarkrishna, after a sizeable visit in the West toward the close of the nineteenth century, noted the West's fierce penchant for planning. He declared that as long as Western people were as overplanned as they insisted on being, no authentic spiritual movement could ever come out of the West!

This "spiritual substance" of India reveals itself again in the way certain needs of the spirit are taken for granted in their very naturalness, their "of course-ness." If after a villager bathes in the village tank at the break of day, he should sit quietly under a tree for half an hour to collect himself for the day, nobody thinks of him as strange. When a medical doctor in Almora goes off for a month of meditation in the Himalayas and puts up a notice telling what he has gone off to do and refers his patients to a colleague who will take his practice while he is gone, no one suspects him of hiding a nervous breakdown. When men or women reach the final third of their lives in classical Hindu practice, they are encouraged to withdraw from the active responsibilities they had hitherto borne in the family and the community, and to use this time for the deeper ordering of the soul. Far from being thought of as copping out of life, their little forest centers or ashrams, with enough of a garden to support a simple life, were sought out by those in active life as places to seek counsel and refreshment. There is a classical Asian expression: "Stillness is returning to one's roots." And for India, it has been said that it would not be an exaggeration to say that Nature considers each person important enough to require stillness—in its full meaning of openness to the unplanned flow of life.

The Taoists of China have classically been the spokesmen for the unplanned life, for the unstructured capacity to let life flow through us and not to impede its movement by our rigidly contrived blockages, and they have called upon nature as their guide and sponsor. But nature, too, has her planned seasons. The sun rises and sets. And every form of life has its requirement to make a continuous exchange with its environment: to take in and to give out. If we are to probe as well as to be probed by these Asian strictures on planning, it raises the question of whether planning is the real barrier or whether it is, instead, the driven, frantic, St. Vitus sort of twisted planning that leaves out or largely neglects the encouragement of the deepest exchange of all: those exchanges that true leisure and contemplation enhance, exchanges that take place when we have returned to our roots.

May Sarton in her *Plant Dreaming Deep* speaks of the true planning and of the false planning. "I knew from having watched my father in his farm work how supportive a routine is, how the spirit moves around freely in it. Routine is not a prison, but the way into freedom from time. The apparently measured time has immeasurable space in it, and in this it resembles music. . . . The routine I established in my early days has remained much the same. It revolves around the early morning hours at my desk, then moves gradually into the rest of the house."

Of the false planning, she says, "I began to understand that for me 'waste' had not come from idleness, but perhaps from pushing myself too hard, from not being idle enough, from listening to the demon that says make haste. I had allowed the wrong kind of pressure to build up . . . I was helped by Louise Bogan's phrase 'Let life do it' . . . learning to let the day shape the work."

It is interesting to a Quaker to explore the remark from several sides. For there is a sense in which the Friends who have kept to the initial thrust of the Quaker movement, although they are themselves an interiorized form of the Christian witness, have nevertheless throughout their history been in continuous protest against an over-planned church, with overplanned programs, overplanned rituals, overplanned physical plants, overplanned creedal requirements, and overplanned authority and patterns of governance. Believing that Christ is come to teach his people himself, they have gathered in unplanned and unprogrammed services of silent worship, in plain, unadorned buildings, trusting to the Spirit to operate in their close lay community. They rely heavily on working collectively day by day on the personal concerns and tasks which the Inward Guide in this return to their roots may have laid upon them. Of this Inward Guide, the Quakers would agree with Thomas Merton that when they are truly quiet and centered "we don't have to rush after it. It was there all the time and if we give it time, it will make itself known to us."

These individual concerns may eventually quicken the consciousness of the whole group and they may find corporate ways of implementing them. Yet these concerns are generally initiated in the heart of some individual member.

In reply to a question of a person in a Canadian audience who asked him for a single practical hint of a way to resolve a problem that he faced, the late Eric Fromm is reported to have answered with a single word, "Quietness." After a pause, he went on to say, "The experience of stillness—you have to stop in order to change direction."

Many of the admonitions that are found in the writings of such trusted Quaker guides as George Fox or William Penn would underline Eric Fromm's contemporary rediscovery of this quietness, this contemplative climate of inward leisure in which these occasions of "turning around" so often take place.

George Fox says: "Be still and cool in thy own mind and spirit from thy own thoughts and then thou wilt feel the principle of God to turn thy mind . . . thou wilt receive his strength and power from whence life comes to allay all tempests, against blusterings and storms. That is it which molds up into patience, into innocency, into soberness, into stillness, into stayedness, into quietness, into God and his power" (*Epistles,* 1658).

"There is the Danger and Temptation to you of drowning your minds into your business and clogging them with it, so that you can hardly do anything in the service of God but there will be a crying, my business, my business, and your minds will go into things and not over things . . . that Mind that is cumbered, it will fret, being out of the Power of God" (*Epistles,* 1656).

John Woolman is not the only Friend who has taken Fox's word to heart and has coped with this drivenness and with the expectations of his generation for increasing his own and his family's prosperity. Woolman's trimming of his own business and his refusal of several offers of a part in enterprises that looked profitable because "there appeared too great a share of cumber to attend to it" has given a clue that has not been lost on those generations that have followed him.

"Wait to know the time of Silence that quiets all strife" (*Epistles,* 1656), says Fox, and William Penn speaks in a like vein, "Love silence, even in the mind . . . Much speaking, as of thinking, spends, and in many thoughts, as well as words, there is sin. True silence is the rest of the mind; and is to the spirit, what sleep is to the body, nourishment and refreshment" (*Advice to his Children,* 1699).

These admonitions and the principle of order to which they all point could be gathered up in a single testimony that is to be found in the *Imitation of Christ:* "He in whom the Eternal word speaks is delivered from many opinions."

In a little book that was translated under the title *The World of Silence,* the Swiss recluse Max Picard expresses with singular power the cleft in the modern soul that cries out for healing. One of the most poignant warnings that the book contains is that our noise-packed, contemporary world was pocked with *Zusammenlösigkeit*—discontinuousness, lack of any accepted structure. Pascal would have put it in terms of a want of any principle of order that could show the relatedness to each other of the different worlds in which we live.

How else than by a process of almost schizophrenic discontinuity can you explain a society where a man or woman can spend his or her working life making things in which he or she has no interest whatever in where the raw materials come from or to whom the product goes or whether it will enhance or destroy or encumber or decay those who will use it? How else can you explain the internal worlds of colonialism where in a country like South Africa or in areas of our own country, two worlds exist—one for the black and one for the white—and where they are separated from each other only by transparent but all too real curtains, curtains which the ruling group seems to have no serious expectation of removing. How else can you explain a nation that rears its children in nursery schools, grammar schools, and high schools, with its whole educational apparatus devoted to sensitizing those children to a reverence for life in all of its forms, and then at age eighteen seeks to recruit them into training camps where guerilla tactics of the most incredible gruesomeness are taught and where in this total reversal, the whole moral weight of national patriotism is thrown behind the butchering of those who are designated as the "current enemy?" How can men and women continue to live in a world where its religious forces have abandoned national boundaries, where its scientific forces cut across every national and even ideological boundary, and yet go on clinging to the notion of operating in an absolutely sovereign national state that even refuses to promise in advance to abide by the decisions of the World Court?

A contemplation that will seek a principle of order that will challenge these anarchies and these dissonances must not, however, be a phony. Our world will not tolerate that. It must be a penetration that goes so deep that it reaches through to a principle of order that will draw these conflicting areas into a common responsibility. This contemplation, which is the capacity to see through the specious claims to absolute autonomy, and to grasp the underlying principle of order, is a costly business. Ruskin once declared, "The greatest thing the human soul ever does in this world is to see something and tell what it saw in a plain way. Hundreds of people can talk for one who can think, but thousands can think for one who can see. To see clearly is poesy and prophecy and religion in one."[11]

How have the great men and women of history used this gift of contemplation? Perhaps the greatest master of contemplation of the early middle ages was Bernard of Clairvaux. When one of his fellow Cistercians was chosen as Pope Eugenius III, Bernard of Clairvaux sent him some plain counsel. In it, he advised him to take time to cultivate this gift of *seeing*. It is counsel on "how to abound," how to bear prosperity and not to be its victim, how to wield power responsibly, how to penetrate through this veil of *Zusammenlösigkeit* and grasp the common principle of order. In the passage that follows, note that the word "consideration" is almost synonomous with what is here called contemplation.

Bernard counsels Eugenius III "not to give yourself up altogether nor at all times to the active life but to set aside some time for consideration. . . . Is anything in all respects so influential as consideration? Does it not by kindly anticipation create the divisions of the active life itself in a manner rehearsing and arranging beforehand what has to be done? Consideration purifies the very fountain that is the mind from which it springs. Then it governs the affections, corrects excesses, softens the manners, adorns and regulates the life, and bestows the knowledge of things divine and human alike. It is consideration which in prosperity feels the sting of adversity, in adversity is as though it felt it not."[12]

It is interesting to think of Thomas More, when he was Lord High Chancellor of England and Henry VIII's chief minister, spending one day of each week in his little Chelsea summerhouse at the foot of his garden that ran down to the Thames, engaged in meditation, in reading, in reflecting, in writing, in order to pierce through to the principle of order both for his own life and for that of his country.

Anker Larsen, a Danish mystic whom Rufus Jones always admired and with whom I once spent a day at his home in a suburb of Copenhagen a long generation ago, suggests in the closing pages of his spiritual autobiography *With the Door Open,* that "the most comprehensive formula for human culture which I know was given by the old peasant who, on his death bed, obtained from his son only this one promise: to sit every day for half an hour *alone* in the best room. The son did this and became a model for the whole district. This father's command had taken thought for everything, for Eternity, soul-deepening, refinement, history."[13]

Now if we are to look at the naked act of contemplation itself, there is a sense in which we do not even have to justify it by regarding it as an antidote for the *Zusammenlösigkeit* disease. Contemplation is self-justifying. It is good in itself. The fourteenth-century writer of the *Cloud of Unknowing* has a moving passage on this most human and yet most eternal role of the gift to man of contemplation: "The condition of the active life is such that it is both begun and ended in this life. This is not so of the contemplative life; it is begun in this life and it shall last forever and ever."[14] Contemplation is a gift that makes a person human and needs show no other fruits for its justification. Because I am a person, I am potentially a contemplative animal and that is all there is to it.

Yet when I look at the nature of contemplation, I discover certain broad features of it that affect the world of those who carry it out, and we must now look at these. Plotinus placed contemplation in a metaphysical setting that we need not accept in all of its detail in order to grasp the genius of what he wished to share with us about this most human of activities. He saw two great movements taking place: the one was the movement in creation by which the One, the ground of all Being, donated to all things their being. The other was the process of contemplation by which the created beings come awake, and by reflecting on their source, move back again to the One from whom they came and draw the lower orders along with them. Here is the recovery in gratitude of a principle of order, of an inner relatedness, of compassion, of love that would restore that Zusammenheit—that togetherness that Picard declares our world has lost. Here is a new angle of vision. Here is the double vision that Blake proclaims and the end of "single vision and Newton's sleep." Here is the kind of thing that made John Woolman feel that he was mixed inextricably with all suffering humanity and made Eugene Debs declare that "while any man is in prison, I am not free." Yet here is the togetherness that refuses to accept any claim to an ultimate and absolute autonomy that science or economics or politics or art may make. It sees them all as connected, all as responsible to help man in this return movement, all as under this principle of order, all as responding to an invisible beat. This is one major movement of genuine contemplation.

Closely related to this sense of responsible togetherness and yet seeming to be its absolute antithesis is the gift which real contemplation possesses of seeing things as they are in themselves and helping to preserve the holy angularity of things from any reductionist forces that are forever trying to crowd them into their molds. Loren Eiseley, the gifted anthropologist whose *Immense Journey* and *The Mind as Nature* have provoked a fresh sense of wonder in the hearts of so many, has been throughout an advocate for the irreducibility of the wild, the unpredictable, the freshly original character in things that gives them their individuality. Let me quote two snatches from an unpublished lecture of his, *Creativity and Modern Science,* which Eiseley gave to a group made up largely of scientists: "Perhaps, after all, a world so created has something still wild and unpredictable lurking behind its more sober manifestations. It is my contention that this is true and that the rare freedom of the particle to do what most particles never do is duplicated in the solitary universe of the human mind." Again he says, "It is through the individual brain that there passes the momentary illumination in which the whole human countryside may be transmuted in an instant." "A steep and unaccountable transition," Thoreau has described it, "from what is called a common sense view of things, to an infinitely expanding and liberating one, from seeing things as men describe them, to seeing them as men cannot describe them." This capacity of the contemplative mind to do what Shelley called stripping the veil of familiarity from things is what enables the contemplative to play a peculiar role in policing the precincts of human consciousness and of protecting this precious, holy angularity and making sure that its integrity is respected.

It is not alone the poet G. M. Hopkins who can cry out "Glory be to God for dappled things," for the true contemplative lifts into glory the surd in us and in nature that can never be reduced. G. K. Chesterton in a letter to his fiancée in 1899, which is quoted by Maisie Ward, writes, "I am black but comely at this moment because the cyclostyle has blacked me. . . . I like the cyclostylic ink; it is so inky. I do not think there is anyone who takes quite such fierce pleasure in things being themselves as I do. The startling wetness of water excites and intoxicates me; the fieriness of fire, the steeliness of steel, the unutterable muddiness of mud."[15]

Always the gift of contemplation returns this capacity to see things as they are and to insist that any attempt at grasping an ultimate unity in things must be achieved only after there is the deepest reverence given to the untamable mystery in all things. There is a Hasidic story told of a son who had taken his father's place, on his death, as the rabbi of the community, and after a time a member of the community came and complained that he was doing things very differently from his father and that the community was dissatisfied with the changes. The son denied this and insisted that he was doing exactly as his father had done. "My father imitated nobody, and I imitate nobody!"

Whether it is a religious contemplative or a writer like Pasternak, this untamable originality in the universe can never be extinguished and the contemplative spirit both seeks and discloses a principle of order at the very same time that it witnesses to the character of shiningness in the "stones along the road, that are and cannot be."

Even the contemplative's speech is not unaffected. Wittgenstein once counselled that it may be well simply "to point" where we may not exhaustively describe, and the contemplative has long been doing exactly this in recording the fruits of contemplation. John Woolman's *Journal* records a word which an old Indian, Chief Papunehang, spoke to Woolman through his interpreter after a silent meeting for worship in which John Woolman had risen to pray but had not used an interpreter. Referring to this prayer that had been made in English and that he had therefore not understood, Papunehang said, "I love to feel where words come from." Speech that is big with that which is beyond speech and that feels the immensity and richness that requires some freshly minted expression to carry it, always has something clinging to it. "Half his strength he gave not forth," and speech that has come out of the silence and out of contemplation so often has a way of helping us to feel that unused reserve.

The fruits of contemplation have been expressed very differently but they seem, each in its own way, to be rimmed with this gift of pointing. If someone had asked Albert Schweitzer what he had learned during his first decades in Africa, he might have replied in this mood of pointing, "Nothing much, just reverence for life."

As I indicated at the outset, this long look at the function of contemplation in the nature of man cannot be considered as a digression in any examination of the nature of leisure. Joseph Pieper, whose essay on *Leisure, the Basis of Culture* is still considered the most penetrating treatment of the subject, suggests that true leisure is to be found only in a certain temper of the human spirit. It is a quality of inner spaciousness, of inner receptivity, of inward collectedness.

I find it almost impossible to see how one could improve upon Joseph Pieper's own words.

> Leisure implies (in the first place) an attitude of non-activity, of inward calm, of silence; it means not being "busy," not letting things

happen. . . . Leisure is a form of silence, of that silence that is the pre-requisite of the apprehension of reality: only the silent hear and those who do not remain silent, do not hear. Silence as it is used in this context, does not mean "dumbness" or "noiselessness": it means more nearly that the soul's power to "answer" to the reality of the world is left undisturbed. For leisure is a receptive attitude, and it is not only the occasion but also the capacity for steeping oneself in the whole of creation.[16]

If there is anything that differentiates this description of true leisure from the account that I have given of the nature and the need for contemplation, it is in the pitting of leisure against activity, against drivenness, against strain, against compulsive busyness. Yet even the damping down of these inward conditions would seem to me to be simply preparatory measures for contemplation; to be wise counsels for a kind of emptying; a slipping out of the grip of our world's fierce artificial respiration. They are ways for restoring in us the interior space that is meant to be there, of giving us a wider margin around the page. These aspects give an interior dimension to the empty spaces of time, to what Webster calls "periods of unengaged time," that it is customary to use in defining leisure.

When Joseph Pieper moves on to define what these preparatory states should lead to and speaks of their clearing of the way for "the soul's power to 'answer' to the reality of the world," he has left the empty spaces and now is speaking precisely of the deep, intuitive action of the human spirit that I have tried to describe as contemplation. He even speaks of this as a "contemplative attitude" so that all distinction between the two is removed and it becomes clear that he is at bottom defining true leisure as a form of contemplation. In so doing it appears that there is no longer a necessity to pit emptiness against activity or to confine this temper of the human spirit to "non-activity."

In the "answer" that I make there may be both a profound peace beyond all agitation and yet the most intense activity. The fourteenth-century English mystics speak freely of "the rest most busyee." For now the activity is an answering of the soul to both the disclosure and to the unfathomable mystery of that to which it is exposed, and this may cover the whole spectrum of our relation with nature, with each other, and with what undergirds them both. Thomas Merton once spoke of our being open to receive glints of "the mysterious unity and integrity, the invisible fecundity, a dimmed light, a meek hidden wholeness," that is in all things. Again he suggests, "There is in all things an inexhaustible sweetness and purity, a silence, that is the fountain of action and joy. It rises as if in a wordless gentleness and flows out to me from unseen roots in all created being."[17]

This "fountain of action and joy" and this "hidden wholeness" is in all things, and therefore is inherently accessible to all persons. It is a public good. The capacity to answer to it is not reserved for the inactive. It may be experienced in the thick of heavy responsibility. It is not necessarily found in those who teach philosophy, or confined to any occupation, or to those who are completely free of designated work. It is not reserved for youth or for the venerable. It may be present in monasteries or may live in families. In spite of Thoreau and John Muir, it is not given only to country dwellers and denied to urban man. It is rather a quality of approach to any situation, an inwardly spacious way of being present and open to where we are.

It is perfectly clear that some practices and some cultures do encourage it and that others are given to its neglect. Yet the spirit of man is such that no culture or society is ever without some persons and usually some cultural islands where inhabitants have made and are making these discoveries and who continue to keep these options open to us all.

A decade before his death in 1941, Henri Bergson gave us his too little explored spiritual testament, *The Two Sources of Morality and Religion.* In its closing chapter, he called attention to the great technological resources of our age which could, if properly mobilized, conquer the elemental needs of all persons on the globe in our time, and even in the foreseeable time. He then accented two points: The first was that because these elemental physical needs of persons could actually be met, we were in a position, for the first time in the world's history, to have a "clean" contemplation. What he meant was that up to that time there was always a suspicion that man contemplated and turned away from the foreground of life when life was too much for him, and that his contemplation might always be accused of being a form of life-flight from the agony of realizing that every tenth or every third neighbor must die before his time because of the shortage of food or the ravages of uncontrolled disease. Contemplation could, therefore, never fully clear itself from the accusation of being a kind of cop-out. Now, Bergson insisted, contemplation need no longer be haunted by such a shadow.

His second word to his time was that only contemplation and a greater soul could pierce the temptation of those who presently control the technological apparatus to fail the deprived peoples of the earth, and to go on sequestering the vast new increments of wealth for themselves alone. Unless the nurture of a great ground swell of contemplation can overcome the split in consciousness, the *Zusammenlösigheit* of our epoch, the masters of the technological apparatus, Bergson believes, will forfeit this new promise and this mutation will be muted.

True leisure and true contemplation on all its levels is a condition of the human spirit that needs no social justification for its practice. Yet it is hard to see how one could exaggerate the human stakes that are involved in its return to strength in our time.

Notes

1. *Centuries of Meditations* (London: Dobell, 1927), Part I, p. 22.
2. *Summa Theologica* (London: Burns, Oates and Washburne, 1922), Part 2, Sec. 180, Art. 3.
3. *On Contemplation,* trans. Blanche Shaffer, *Friends World News,* No. 16, 1945, p. 1.
4. Ibid.
5. *Markings* (New York: Knopf, 1964), p. 89.
6. *Surrender* (Morehouse, N.Y., 1931), p. 21.
7. *A Philosophy of Solitude* (New York: Simon and Schuster, 1933), p. 163.
8. *Philosophy of Form* (London: Grant Richards, 1920), p. 241.
9. *Practical Mysticism* (New York: E. P. Dutton, 1915), p. 11.
10. *Mysticism* (London: Methuen, 1911), p. 532.
11. *Modern Painters,* Vol. III, Part IV, Chapter 16.
12. Bernard of Clairvaux, *On Consideration,* trans. C. Lewis (Oxford: Clarendon, 1908), I,7.
13. (New York: Macmillan, 1931), pp. 100–101.

14. *Cloud of Unknowing* (New York: Harper, 1948), p. 14.
15. *Gilbert Keith Chesterton* (New York: Sheed and Ward, 1943), pp. 108–109.
16. *Leisure, the Basis of Culture* (London: Faber and Faber, 1952), p. 52.
17. Quoted in the foreword to Thomas Merton's *A Hidden Wholeness.*

EIGHT

The Mystical Experience

P ascal in his *Thoughts* has an insistent plea for attacking things in
the right order and adds, "This order consists chiefly in digressions
on each point to indicate the end, and to keep it always in sight."[1] The
"end" of this inquiry would seem to me to be to consider how we are
to assess the legitimacy and the significance for religion, for ethics, for
philosophy, and for culture of the substantial body of human experience down through the ages which has been called "mystical" and
which has claimed to have had direct and immediate touch with what
is regarded as ultimate reality. I hope to pay particular attention to
the intellectual and anti-intellectual aspects of this experience and its
interpretation. But these aspects are so interwoven with this cluster
of problems that I want at least to set forth at the outset that I would
ask you to grant me the right to make a few of these Pascalian
"digressions," hoping to be able to keep the end "always in sight" and
not to neglect at least some few facets of my assignment before I have
finished.

Unresolved Problems

Can the Mystic Communicate his Experience?

Let us, then, look at some of the unresolved problems that confront
us in this field of the relation of mysticism to religion, to ethics, to
philosophy and to culture. While not unique to mysticism, as the
poets and novelists know all too well, there is, nevertheless, the problem of the relation of the mystical experience itself to the very language in which the communicating mystic expresses this experience.
Someone has defined language as "crystallized psychology." If this
phrase is apt, it is, however, only to refer to the canon of language as

having been largely closed when the reports of the senses and of intellectual abstractions were deemed to be in. If it is true that language is so much the product of this limited but extremely vivid segment of human experience, how, then, is it possible to express in its ceramic molds an experience that claims to be neither sensory in origin nor to be an intellectual abstraction? Or if it has conformed itself to such limitations, how accurate or how adequate an account of the mystical experience is it capable of presenting? Henri Bergson in a related context has wrestled valiantly with this very problem.

When such a mystic as Meister Eckhart declares that "words are interlopers between ourselves and God"[2] is he referring only to vocal prayer or to this broader problem? Closely meshed with this problem, although containing other issues, is the whole matter of Negative Theology as an attempt to express the mystical dilemma of communicating in a language that was not thrown up to express what it has touched.

What is the Role of the Vehicle or Tradition in which the Mystic Stands?

A second issue that is closely allied with the problem of language is the influence upon the very nature of the mystical experience itself which may have been exerted by the religious and cultural traditions in which the mystics have been reared. Has this religious and cultural tradition affected the very nature of the mystical experience? Has it affected the way in which it has been interpreted? Has it aroused a climate of expectancy that such mystical disclosures may take place? This vehicle of the tradition in which the mystic stands needs the most searching scrutiny, for within its scope there are clustered a whole aggregate of problems for mysticism if we dare to venture into making any comparisons between the mystics of the Christian West, the mystics of Judaism, of Islam, of Hinduism, of Buddhism, to say nothing of those curious crossings of these traditions which different historical periods have presented.

Why do mystics of these different traditions differ in their experience of the nature of ultimate reality? Why do some find in their most intimate touch with this ultimate reality a complete negation of the world of creation in favor of a transpersonal universe of cosmic peace and an accompanying negation of the integral center of their personal identity, while others find their touch with a One who supports the creation and the values of creation, transcending them but transcending them in their direction, and who, far from extinguishing the personal center, on the contrary, find this very personal center flooded and enhanced in a whole spectrum of ways?

Autistic and Other-Directed Mysticism

A third and closely allied problem is the mystery of why some mystics find themselves absorbed and completely satisfied to spend the balance of their days in seeking further renewals of their experience, while others find themselves restored to the world of creation by what has happened to them, and restored with a vast enhancement of their volitional powers to serve their fellows in this world? Is this drastic difference due to the religious and cultural tradition in which the mystic was brought up and in which he or she stands when the experience is over? Is it due to the mystic's psychological type? Is it due to the depth of the mystical experience itself? Is it due to the degree of subsequent yielding within the mystic to the Ground to which the experience has witnessed? If the mystical experience is a genuine disclosure of the nature of ultimate reality, why, then, should these widely admitted differences exist?

Natural and Theistic Mysticism

A fourth nest of problems center around the focussing more specifically upon the differences that appear between theistic and nontheistic or natural mysticism, as it is called by some, and which may involve "a feeling of oneness with the universe as a whole, a sense of the illusive character of life, and an experience of being emancipated from the temporal and material world as in listening to a Beethoven symphony" but with little reference to or interest in the character of that with which I may have felt this oneness. The most able Roman Catholic interpreters of mysticism, men like Zaehner and de Lubac, would find this distinction between theistic and natural mysticism something that was fairly self-evident and able to be sustained. Zaehner, for instance, in his *Mysticism: Sacred and Profane,* finds this distinction highly useful not only in dealing with the chemically induced mystical states that Aldous Huxley has championed in his *Doors of Perception,* but also in distinguishing the higher levels of mysticism from the very widespread undergirding of natural mysticism that he acknowledges, but that he sees transcended in theistic mysticism. This distinction would be rejected by some interpreters of mysticism who seek to show that all mysticism is reductive of differences that exist or of any such notion of "levels," and who affirm that any differences in mystical experience can be accounted for by external means and need not be taken as seriously discrediting the basic unit of the mystical witness.

Can Mysticism be Induced or Acquired?

A fifth area in these problems that needs close attention is the issue that was referred to above in connection with chemically induced mental states which may have certain similarities to the mystical experience. It is the more general question of whether genuine mystical states can ever be induced at all, either by inner means of preparation for them or by external means of stimulating them. Are they ever subject to human manipulation, or are they not rather to be regarded as gifts of grace that come from beyond and come without previous effort or merit, or at least quite independently of them? Closely related to this problem is the question of whether the mystical life is open to all, or whether it is a gift bestowed only on a few? Perhaps a third possibility may also be included among these alternatives and that is that all human beings have some basic disclosures of a mystical nature in the course of their lives; that this may be regarded as a given in the *condition humaine,* as an underpinning of all consciousness; but that the enhancement of this in a major way may well be the gift of a few, and further, that those who are also able to set it down in such a way as to make it convincing to others may be restricted to a still smaller band.

Has Mysticism an Intellectual Role in Ethics, Religion, and Philosophy?

A final problem, among those I mean to take note of, appears when we try to relate the mystical experience to ethics, to religion, to culture, and to philosophy and to see what its implications are for these areas.

In ethics, society may be suspicious of the mystical element and of its ecumenical accents on more inclusive responsibilities for its fellows, an accent that may even fling the cloak of tenderness and concern over the momentary public enemies. An ethical thinker like the late Nicolai Hartmann rejected the whole of the religious dimension, fearing that it might in some way envelop and dissolve away the firm vertebrate structure of the delicate hierarchy of values which he, as an ethicist, had built up with great labor and pains. He was taking no chances on the possibility that mystical religion's "Love God and do as you please" might manage to plunge man's moral sense into subjective chaos.

In religion, the institutional and historical forms of religion, including its revealed scriptures as well as the theological and intellectual formulations of its beliefs, appear as its hereditary custodians that are often as grim and forbidding as the sculptured forms of the ferocious and heavily armed temple guardians that stand in the outer portals of a Thai Buddhist temple toward the admission of this mystical element, which may well have an upsetting effect upon their traditional order.

As to the relationship with the given culture at large, this block of experience of the ultimate, if it is not to be dismissed as private, subjective, or even illusory, would have to show how it was a genuine formative force in the culture in order to be valued. If it was a means of eluding further touch with the balance of the culture, it might be rejected as "life-flight" or as an allergy to the customary values by which the culture was sustained and regarded as some kind of cultural disease whose pathology needed study. A figure like Spengler would almost certainly find in mysticism and its claims a sign of decadence and of the approaching withering touch of a wintry death for that culture.

On the philosophical front, the query could at once be made as to whether the mystic (with his declarations of how sublime beyond describing the beholder had found the vision or the union with the ultimate) really had anything to say at all and whether if he did it would have to be disqualified and stripped of all truth claims and set down as apparently a highly satisfying subjective experience that some people enjoy, and stop at that point.

The Contributions of Mysticism to Ethics, Religion, Culture, and Philosophy

It is in the area of this sixth set of problems that I may now be able to undertake my assignment of discussing whether mysticism is basically intellectual or anti-intellectual and how it is to be weighed out in its contributions to ethics, to religion, to culture, and to philosophy. But it must be clear that all of the groups of problems that I have dealt with will continually hover over and query any judgments that I may seek to make in this more limited area, so that it is quite impossible from time to time not to digress and to touch on some of them as I proceed; and that to do so is not to cease to keep the proper "end in sight."

I should say at the outset that I shall take my examples almost exclusively from the Christian tradition with which I am most familiar. While this will limit me in one sense, it is a broad and a rich enough tradition to illustrate nearly all of the problems that we are discussing.

Some Dimensions of the Mystical Encounter

I can hardly deal with the implications of mysticism for ethics, religion, culture, and philosophy, without some direct description of the experience itself, and there my first "diversion" will deal with the issue of whether mysticism can be induced or acquired. I think that the first feature that marks the testimony of the Christian mystical experience is its witness to the ravishing, energizing, quickening power of the order that impinges upon our own and that in the mystical breakthrough gives such an inexpressible delight and refreshment to the soul. There are few more eloquent passages in mystical literature that express this than Bernard of Clairvaux's word to his Cistercian brothers that is found in his Sermons on the Canticle of Canticles:

> I confess then, that the Word has visited me and even very often. But although He has frequently entered into my soul, I have never at any time been sensible of the precise moment of His coming. I have felt that He was present: I remember that He has been with me; I have sometimes been able even to have a presentiment that He would come; but never to feel His coming or His departure. For

when He came to enter my soul, or whither He went on quitting it, by what means He has made entrance or departure, I confess that I know not even to this day . . . You will ask then, how, since the ways of His access are thus incapable of being traced, I could know that He was present: But He is living and full of energy, and as soon as He has entered into me, He has quickened my sleeping soul, has aroused and softened and goaded my heart, which was in a state of torpor and hard as a stone. He has begun to pluck up and destroy, to plant and to build, to water the dry places, to illuminate the gloomy spots, to throw open those which were shut close, to inflame with warmth those which were cold, as also to straighten its crooked paths and make its rough places smooth, so that my soul might bless the Lord and all that was within me bless His Holy Name . . . it was not by His motions that He was recognized by me . . . It was only by the movement of my heart, that I was enabled to recognize His presence, and to know the might of His power by the sudden departure of vices and the strong restraint put on the carnal affections. From the discovery and conviction of my secret faults I have had good reason to admire the depths of His wisdom; His goodness and kindness have become known in the amendment, whatever it may amount to, of my life; while in the reformation and renewal of the spirit of my mind, that is of my inward man, I have perceived in some degree the loveliness of His beauty, and have been filled with amazement at the multitude of His greatness as I meditated on these things . . . But when the Word withdrew Himself, all spiritual powers and faculties began to droop and languish. It was as though the fire had been removed from under a bubbling kettle. Such to me is the sign of departure.[3]

The feature in this passage from Bernard of Clairvaux of the coming and the going of the mystical experience should be noted, for almost nowhere in mystical literature is there any claim that it is more than a passing (John of the Cross calls it a "transient") disclosure. This should not surprise us, for our human consciousness never seems capable of holding any experience for more than a brief span of time, and, although repeatable, each event inevitably fades out after its interval is spent. The beatific vision, which expresses in the Christian tradition the place and role of the mystical gift, has never in this life been claimed to give us more than an anticipatory and fleeting glimpse of what in another existence, it is hoped, may be continuous.

In his *Adornment of the Spiritual Marriage,* the Flemish mystic, Jan Ruysbroeck, refers to the delight and the sense of instant newness of this feature of the repeatability of the experience.

> The coming of the Bridegroom is so swift that He is always come and is always dwelling within us with all His riches; and ceaselessly and ever and again. He is coming in His own person with new clarity, just as if He never were come before. For to come consists in an eternal now, without time, which is constantly received in new joy and delight.[4]

But, as with our common sense realism that philosophers build upon in interpreting our sense perceptions, there is little inclination to interpret this episodic chain of experiences as other than brought about by the limitations of the subject's apparatus of apprehension; so also with the mystic, there is the assumption that the Giver of the mystical experience is continually present. It is we who are not always there, and it is believed to be the subject and its variously interpreted limitations that fail to record this continuity. Fénelon's word expresses the mystic's testimony, "The wind of God is always blowing, but you must hoist your sail."

Some Christian mystics are more avid than others in describing the continuity of the source of the mystical experience and the eagerness of the yearning of this source to spill out its love into the subject. In a tradition not alien to the Timaeus's account of the impetus of the initial act of creation as being a quality of goodness in the source that impelled it to share this largess, these Christian mystics add to this the Christian witness that there is One who "stands at the door and knocks" and in such a spokesman as Meister Eckhart proclaim boldly and without reservation that the very nature of God is to give of himself.

> God is foolishly in love with us. It seems he has forgotten heaven and earth and all his happiness and deity; his entire business seems with me alone, to give me everything to comfort me; he gives it to me suddenly, he gives it to me wholly, he gives it to me perfect, he gives it all the time, and he gives it to all creatures.[5]

Eckhart's figures get even more raucous and unguarded in a later sermon when he compares God to a horse rolling in a field.

It is like a horse turned loose in a lush meadow giving vent to his horse-nature by galloping full tilt about the field: he enjoyes it and it is his nature. And just in the same way, God's joy and satisfaction in his likes find vent in his pouring his entire nature and his being into this likeness, for he is this likeness himself.[6]

But if this burgeoning of divine love is seeking its likeness in every man and is spilling itself Niagara-like over each soul, why, then, are so few made aware of this colossal donation? Eckhart's answer is swiftly given. We are too elsewhere. We are not at home in our own souls. We are "cut off outside ourselves." The *Imitation of Christ* says that "all want peace, but they do not want the things that lead to true peace." There must, then, be some final act of will, of consent, on our part, that the heavenly visitant requires before his torrent of grace is unleashed. Eckhart maintains stoutly that "God is found to act, to pour himself out into thee as soon as ever he shall find thee ready. . . . He longs for thee a thousand-fold more urgently than thou for him: one point the opening and the entering."[7] God cannot leave anything void and unfilled.

But the very human business of the making of the void, of the spiritual "space" for the mystical torrent to enter, how is this to be done, and why do any tarry? Eckhart's answer is here in the great mystical tradition in placing the fear of the cost of purgation, the fear of the relentless demands of perfect attention, the fear of what "the entering" will bring about if "the opening" is made. Eckhart is blunt. "The Kingdom of God is for the perfectly dead," and knowingly he observes that "There are plenty to follow our Lord half way, but not the other half. . . . We would fain be humble; but not despised. . . . We would be poor but without privation and doubtless we are patient, except with hardships and with disagreeables."[8]

Is the Mystical Experience a Sheer Gift of Grace?

Is the mystical experience, then, something that we acquire by the courage of our yielding? Is it less a matter of Grace and more like a decoration of the Purple Heart, a merit badge for those wounded in this battle of the soul? This issue has always been a hardy perennial among the mystics and the interpreters of mysticism. John of the Cross is more delicate and restrained in interpreting it. For him it is rather described from within the mystical experience, described as its concomitant, described as what Grace does to a soul that it invades. The cost is no less than in Eckhart's description, but it is not something done in our own strength prior to the experience. It is done within the experience so that the acquired and the gratuitously given are almost indistinguishable. Implied always is the possibility of my slipping from the surgeon's table, wrenching away from the hand of the divine physician, but John of the Cross's picture is from one who had known both the anaesthesia of being wonderfully brought through the surgery alive, and yet, like Bernard of Clairvaux, of having a dim consciousness of what the surgery had cut away and almost of each step in the process.

John of the Cross speaks reluctantly of "the tender wound in the depth of the soul." "It is hard," he admits, "to speak of that which passes in the depth of the spirit."[9] He uses the figure of fire to represent the spirit and the log for our souls: "The soul that is in a state of transformation of love may be said to be, in its ordinary habit, like the log of wood that is continually assaulted by fire,"[10] and he means to imply that if all conditions are capable of the mystic experience, all "logs" are not equally ready! The pain and suffering that is borne by the soul that is not ready to bear the burning gaze of love has seldom been more vividly expressed. "In the beginning when this spiritual purgation commences, all the Divine Fire is used in drying up and making ready the wood (which is the soul) rather than in giving heat."[11] There is first of all the charring of the log of our hearts—and only then the setting on fire.

> Even as the fire that penetrates to the log of wood is the same that first of all attacked and wounded it with its flame, cleansing and stripping it of its accidents of ugliness until by means of its heat, it had prepared it to such a degree that it could enter and transform it into itself. Neither is it sweet to it, but grievous . . . torment . . . affliction . . . aridities . . . miserable . . . bitter[12]

are all John's ways of describing the charring.

Yet willingly borne, this purgation can lead to the charred log of the human soul becoming almost incandescent and joining the flame that has inflicted the pain of the charring, and John of the Cross depicts the soul as able finally to sing out, "Oh flame of the Holy

Spirit, that so intimately and tenderly dost pierce the substance of my soul and cauterize it with Thy heat . . . flame that is here sweet to the soul that was aforetime bitter to it."[13]

Catherine of Genoa, in describing her initial mystical experience, gives an even more telling description of the agony that accompanied the ecstasy that outflanks all the debate on the acquired versus the given character of the experience, and yet she does not deny the cost of the agony. On a visit to her sister's Augustinian convent where she had gone to confession:

> At the moment when she was on her knees before him, her heart was pierced by so sudden and immense a love for God, accompanied by so penetrating a sight of her miseries and sins and of his goodness that she was near to falling to the ground . . . she saw the offended one as supremely good, the offender quite the opposite. And hence she could not bear to see any part of herself which was not subjected to the divine justice.[14]

George Fox and Jan Ruysbroeck record kindred conclusions on the cost and character of this experience. "He who shows a man his sin is the same that takes it away"[15] and "To be wounded by love is the sweetest feeling and the sharpest pain which anyone may endure. To be wounded by love is to know for certain that one shall be healed."[16]

We may conclude with Ruysbroeck's hint, in this classic controversy over whether the mystical experience can ever be induced or *acquired,* that while the weight is on the side of its being utterly given, that the gift, if it is more than the wonderful moments or the minor ecstacies of what Zaehner and de Lubac call "natural mysticism," must then by its very nature require a willingness for an inward transformation. He adds that the world is indeed full of men "who would like well to receive the solace from God, if they might partake of him without pains and labor."[17]

It would be well to note that the experiences that we have been looking at have come out of the Christian tradition, and that they would all be classifiable as theistic mystics. What was their witness to contribute to the range of religious, ethical, cultural, and philosophical life of their period? Was it a public and intellectually assimilable tradition or was it basically anti-intellectual, private and incommunicable?

Is the Mystical Experience a Regression to an Infranoetic Condition?

If we could range the extreme assessments of this query, we might find George Santayana, of the *Reason and Religion* stage, at least, at one end of the spectrum and men like von Hügel, E. I. Watkin, and William Ernest Hocking at the other. For Santayana, there is nothing culturally positive to be expected from mysticism. It is the enemy of the "life of Reason," of which Santayana is the champion, and it is depicted as being destructive of the important supporting traditional elements of society in religion, in ethics, and in the struggle of the sciences to catalogue matter.

For Santayana, mysticism represents a reversion to an infranoetic condition, a dropping back into an animallike sensualism which betrays all that is significant in human culture. We begin in this animal-sensual identification with our environing world and only by the painful process of progressive disillusionment do we carve out the perceptual structure and the rationally statable value principles by which we both relate to, and distinguish ourselves from, our physical and social world.

> Mysticism is the most primitive of feelings and only visits formed minds in moments of intellectual arrest and dissolution. It can exist in a child, very likely in an animal: indeed to parody a phrase of Hügel's, the only true mystics are the brutes. . . . In the "Life of Reason" it is, if I may say so, a normal disease, a recurrent manifestation of lost equilibrium and interrupted growth. . . . The feelings which in mysticism rise to the surface and speak in their own name . . . are the background of consciousness coming forward and blotting out the scene.[18]

The self-styled "classicists" like Julian Benda, the author of *Belphegor* and *The Treason of the Intellectuals,* or the literary classicists of a generation ago like Irving Babbitt or Paul Elmer More would almost certainly applaud these remarks as would the enthusiasts of "tradition" in almost every culture.

At the other pole could be ranged figures like Baron Friedrich von Hügel or E. I. Watkin or William Ernest Hocking, who look upon the mystic as giving us a direct confirmation of man's highest hopes: in religion by witnessing directly both to the unutterable holiness of the ground of being and to the well of infinite tenderness and love present there that is directly accessible to man and that in the mystical experience has, in an unmediated fashion, moved man's depths; in ethics for the restoration of the inner bond between a man's own life and that of his fellows ("My heart was tender and often contrite, and universal love to my fellow-creatures increased in me"[19]); in philosophy for undergirding man's hope that the all-too-visible cleft between man's knowledge and the real, is ultimately bridgeable, for he, the mystic, has already crossed the cleft, and that each provisional branch of this knowledge, while always remaining provisional, has some ultimate relevancy.

William Ernest Hocking compares the mystic to the chess player figuring out a solution. He does not yet know what the solution is, but knowing the game from the inside, he knows that there *is* a solution. E. I. Watkin, insisting that all bear the lower levels of the mystical experience within them, suggests that for culture "the mystics are the advance guard of the army of the elect. They are the spies who have gone on ahead and entered before death into the promised land to report somewhat of it to their fellow travellers in the desert. For proof they bring us back a cluster of grapes such as never grew in the vineyards of Egypt."[20]

It is not implausible to return to Santayana and to suggest that his genetic account of our knowledge in which any mystical transcending of reason by an adult is to be rejected as a cowardly reversion to the animal sensualism of infantilism may have vastly oversimplified the situation. For, in the course of the development of our ordinary processes of thought, there is surely never any complete dropping away of earlier levels of apprehension, as Santayana implies, but rather a mutual interdependence and coordination of the various levels involved. It is difficult to understand how, unless we dimly know already, the further clarification that knowledge affords would ever be sought after in the first place. And if this is the case, then there must be in the adult process an attempt to recover an ordered connection of our world aided by this dim but early sense that, in spite of the oppositional tension, knower and known belong together. Yet this mature joint action of a gestaltlike sensory perception and the process of discursive thought where we puzzle out connections aspires to and perhaps relies upon having its incomplete efforts gathered up and encouraged not by any reversion to the infranoetic state of infantilism, but by an intuition of a togetherness and kinship with that which they confront that could only be suitably described as a supranoetic state, as one that transcends anything they have yet or are likely soon to reach.

Surely even scientific inquiry relies upon such infranoetic states of an intuition of the whole relationship to lift even its segment of inquiry into a freshly seen whole. When Max Planck says that even physical science has an irrational or mystical element which aids analytic reason,[21] he is certainly not using "mystic" in the full sense of the mystical experience. But he is referring to an upper end of reason, to a supranoetic aspect which might be enormously encouraged and enhanced by the report of the mystic about the accessibility of the ultimate One and, at any rate, that puts the whole process of the transition of knowledge in such a way that the mystic's report is not inevitably consigned to this primitive end of the spectrum. It might be added that it is even conceivable that this primitive end of the spectrum, because it came first, is not necessarily denied some kinship with that which comes later. This is hinted at by a Blake or a Thomas Traherne with their picture of the eye of the child as the truly unclouded eye, or the Benedictine philosopher Trethowan's suggestions, drawn from recent French studies of perception, that from the beginning of life we first perceive the whole scene and only then refine and discriminate within it. But it is not necessary to convict Santayana of having committed the genetic fallacy in order to imply that there are other possibilities than Santayana has suggested for the mystical experience as a witness to encourage the philosophical and scientific process and not to betray it. Perhaps William James in a classic passage has put the matter best of all:

> Our normal working consciousness, rational consciousness we call it, is but one special type of consciousness, whilst all about it, parted from it by the filament of screens, there lie potential forms of consciousness entirely different. We may go through life without suspecting their existence, but supply the requisite stimulus and at a touch, they are there. No account of the universe in its totality can be final which leaves these other forms of consciousness quite disregarded . . . they open up a region though they fail to give a map.

At any rate they forbid a premature closing of accounts with reality.[22]

Is the Negative Theology of the Mystic Anti-intellectual?

As we turn from the dimension of the soul's ravishing delight in the mystical experience and yet simultaneously of the cost to the soul of such an experience, "O burn that searest never, O wound of deep delight," the basic question still remains: does the experience of these classical Christian mystics tell us anything new or significant about the world that would enrich ethics, religion, culture, or philosophy, or is it a strictly private emotional experience which is basically anti-intellectual and incommunicable?

In the documents there is certainly overwhelming evidence that the mystical experience does surpass the categories of philosophy and ethics. Teresa of Avila writes:

> In this state of prayer to which we have now come, there is no feeling but only rejoicing, unaccompanied by any understanding of the thing in which the soul is rejoicing. It realizes that it is rejoicing in some good thing, in which is compressed all good things at once, but it cannot comprehend this good thing. In the rejoicing, all the senses (she clearly uses this term as inclusive of all the human faculties) are occupied so that none of them is free or able to act in any way, inwardly and outwardly.[23]

Meister Eckhart in referring to this being "drowned in the unfathomableness of God" gives an almost identical account:

> This overflowing of the soul causes her higher powers to flood the lower ones and the lower ones to flood the outward man . . . the Divine love-spring surges the soul, sweeping her out of herself into the unnamed being in her original source for that is what God is. Creatures have given him names but in himself he is nameless essence.[24]

Eckhart, like many other mystics, then uses what has been called "Negative Theology" as a way of denying our positive power of expressing adequately the fullness which the mystic has encountered, and unless we can understand what the mystic is saying in this negative theology, we shall miss one of his major contributions to his world. "There is no knowing what God is." Eckhart declares, "Something we do know, what God is not . . ." "By putting names to God the soul is only dressing him up and making a figure of God."[25]

Jan Ruysbroeck confirms Eckhart on this matter of negative theology: "Though the names we give God are many, the most high Nature of God is Simplicity which cannot be named by any creature. But because of his incomprehensible nobility and sublimity which we cannot rightly name nor wholly express, we give him these names."[26] When, however, the mystic, Zaccheus-like, is invited to come down from his tree "for today I must abide at your house,"

> This hasty descent to which he is summoned by God is nothing other than a descent through desire and through love into the abyss of the Godhead which no intelligence can reach in the created light. But where intelligence remains without, desire and longing go in . . . When it loves and rests above all gifts above itself and above all creatures, then it dwells in God and God dwells in it.[27]

John of the Cross joins these witnesses and is quoted by von Hügel in an early essay on *Experience and Transcendence*[28] as saying:

> One of the greatest favors God bestows transiently on the soul in this life is to enable it to see so distinctly and to feel so profoundly that it cannot comprehend him at all. These souls are heroic, in some degree like souls in heaven, where they know him most perfectly and perceive as distinctly as the others that he transcends their vision.

Given this recurring note in classic theistic Christian mysticism, and repudiating, as I think its widely varied recurrences entitle us to repudiate, the suggestion that negative theology is an inherited Plotinian formula that has intruded itself on the Christian mystical experience, what at bottom does it mean? Is it a decisive witness for the anti-intellectual character of all mysticism? Is it an ultimate repudiation of all rational processes in their application to the highest spiritual matters? Is it a repudiation of any ultimate grounding in the realm of man's highest ethical values, or of all significance in traditional culture as a reservoir of these value expectations? To jump hastily to any such conclusion would be, I think, to miss the real message of the mystic's testimony, a message that is only one dimension of what he has to say to us, but is nevertheless a dimension of incalculable importance.

I believe that the mystic is, first of all, concerned to witness to the immeasurable plenitude of what he has encountered: a qualitative Other that is so majestically transcendent, so "given" and not contrived, so over-against him, that it makes any notion of its being a projection of himself, of his own goodness, of his own beauty, a hilarious absurdity. In the second place, it is so full and so rich that, in its presence, all of his cosmic compliments are muted. In the third place, it so overfloods his mental faculties, so absorbs them into the all-encompassing fullness of its ground as to make even distinctions of subject and object fall away and, for the moment at least, to make the Vedic adoration expressed by "wonderful, wonderful, wonderful" seem to be the only appropriate response.

That the mystic is reduced to permanent silence, or that his ethical insights have remained forever after in the dazzling darkness, or that his will and his mental powers have been permanently anesthetized by the experiences which these declarations point to, belies the whole history of the breed. That he or she has something important to say to us about the ultimate nature of things or about ethical values or culture, after this confession of the transcendent character of the ultimate reality that the theistic mystic is free to call God, is never really in question.

William Ernest Hocking once put it well, "It would be far from the truth to say that the mystic's One, because ineffable, is therefore characterless and neutral."[29] "We may refrain from calling the Real 'good' for fear of limiting it to our conceptions of goodness, and yet believe that 'good' comes *nearer* the truth than evil."[30] And far from being agnostic about the ground of all values, the mystic is making an affirmation that the Real infinitely surpasses our values but in their direction. E. I. Watkin in contrasting the agnostic and the mystic insists that, for all of his protests, "the mystic knows that the first cause must be above, not below, its highest effects . . . that Ultimate Reality must be above not below the highest dependent, created being, nor not less than our highest object of knowledge."[31]

John of the Cross is more meticulous than most mystics in describing and interpreting this experience that negative theology is trying to express. In the moment of vision or union, "The soul is made to hear the great Concert of Creation praising its maker." "The soul sees God, by participation, though in reality preserving its own natural substance as distinct from God, although transformed in him."[32] "Yet it is veiled. We still see dimly because all veils are not drawn back."[33]

Here, then, the negative theology always ends by holding together the two ends of the spectrum of the mystical experience. God is cutting-in the soul on the Concert of Creation; yet, although God is ultimately unfathomable in the very fullness of his plenitude, he is not so transcendent as to be inaccessible to men. God in the Concert confirms the highest values of love and purity and singleness of heart as grounded in his radiant nature. Yet there is always the Godhead behind God; always the ineffable; always the sense that all that we draw from experience is at best "veiled knowledge," that it always has an open end. This plenitude and this open end remain. It is out of such an experience that a mystic like Augustine can issue the daring invitation to "love God and do as you (then) please."

Oblique Evidences in the Mystic's Testimony

There is another level of evidences of the mystic's drawing certain conclusions from his experience about the nature of the ultimately real, in spite of his denial that it can ever be plumbed. There are at least three phases of these evidences that are worth noting: 1) The subsequent counsel that the Christian mystic gives to those who would prepare themselves to receive a similar experience; 2) the report of what the experience has done to open the mystic's own life to one set of values and to weaken the grip on him of another set; and 3) the tests that he uses to distinguish a false mystical experience (or one imposed by diabolical powers) from an authentic one.

There is here no direct and incontrovertible evidence that this experience implies the presence in God's nature of qualities akin to the principles that are indicated in the mystic's counsel as to the kind of life that would prepare another to receive this experience of God; or in the magnetic effect upon the highest values in the soul of the beholder ("I found the evil weakening in me and the good raised up")[34] or even in the way in which these effects in the life of the mystic are used as criteria as to the authenticity of the experience as coming from the ultimate reality. But they are hints whose plausibility cannot be ignored if the full sweep of what the mystic has to say about the ultimately real is to be exhaustively searched.

There is no need to repeat the accounts of the purgations that are recommended that were intended to move the soul toward humility, tenderness, and attentive loving openness as ways of preparing it for the mystical visitation, implying that without the soul's willingness to be so transformed there could be no apprehension, no all-embracing visitation by the ultimately real. The second and third aspects of the effect on the soul of such a visitation and the tests of the authenticity of the visitation are so intermingled that they must be considered together.

Teresa of Avila in her famous *Life* speaks of her own way of testing whether a mystical experience that points to a visitation from the ground of holiness is a false or simulated one or a genuine one. She does it in terms of the "jewels," the gifts of life change, that the visitant leaves in her hands.

> And I said I would show them these jewels for all who knew me were well aware how my soul had changed . . . as I had previously been so wicked. I could not believe that if the devil were doing this . . . he would make use of means which completely defeated his own ends by taking away my vices, making me virtuous and strong . . . the soul that has experienced this prayer and this union is left with a very great tenderness of such a kind that it would gladly become consumed not with pain but in tears of joy . . . The position is that when it comes from the devil all this good is hidden from the soul, and flees from it, and the soul becomes restless and peevish . . . the humility left in it is false humility devoid of tranquility and gentleness.[35]

Teresa here is not alone measuring the worth of the experience. She is chiefly insisting that the nature of the jewels left in her hands points to the kind of a Presence that visited her and suggests that this is not an invalid means of identifying him. For one whose nature was tender, loving, and all-caring might be expected to leave one kind of jewels and an impostor another kind. And this she insists she has known at first hand.

Certainly neither these preparatory instructions given by the sea- soned mystics to those who long to expose themselves more fully to the ultimate reality, nor these fruits or jewels or effects that are reported and used as marks of identification of the Giver could ever finally establish with certainty the nature of that which has enraptured the soul. Yet as corroborative and amplifying hints, as short-range criteria, they are highly suggestive.

It would seem right also to add, as a kind of footnote to this previous testimony of the mystics, what now I think would be generally acknowledged but which nevertheless needs to be in the record—that the Christian mystic is able to be distinguished from victims of what was once called "hysteria," to which it was formerly fashionable to consign them. Professor James B. Pratt years ago summed up the case:

> The flabbiness of will and disintegrating of the personality that are so characteristic of the hysterics are certainly the last things to be found in the Christian mystic. In fact, nothing more distinguishes them than just this strength of will, this determination to devote their lives and direct their activities all to this divine purpose.[36]

Von Hügel, in a classical statement about Catherine of Genoa, who, after her mystical transformation, ran a hospital for twenty-five years, holding its staff together through plagues and disasters, says:

> An immense affirmation, an anticipating creative buoyancy and resourcefulness had come full-flood into her and had shifted her center of deliberate interests and willing away from her disordered, pleasure-seeking, sore and sulky self. If the tests of reality in such things are their persistence and large spirituality, applicability and fruitfulness, then something profoundly real and important took place in the soul of that sad and weary woman of six and twenty within that convent chapel at the annunciation tide.[37]

Is the Mystic Friend or Enemy to Ethics, Religion, and Culture?

But the problem of the effects of this mystical experience for the ethical, religious, cultural, and philosophical aspects of any period are still before us. And it is not difficult to see how the tidy ethicist would be shocked by the claim that the mystical experience of overwhelming plenitude and of a ground for mercy and love and tenderness that went beyond any of the clues to these values that men hold in their hands would humiliate him and seem to be a deliberate undermining of both his values and of their authority. When Bergson in his *Two Sources of Morality and Religion* comes to make his description of morality, he cannot restrain himself from building on the rivalry between the "conserving" element in morality and the dangerously inclusive, sensitizing, expanding, tendering dimension of renewal that he links with mystical insight. While in Bergson's account of any aspect of nature no counter tendency is ever completely rejected, there can be no shadow of doubt as to the side which Bergson favors and the enormous weight that he puts upon the mystic's contribution to what he calls "Dynamic Morality."

In the religious field it is no different, for the mystic, with his secure experience of the fathomless ground of love, is always inclined to hold up this as the norm to the absolutization of any one form or shape of the institution, or of the dogmas that may have gotten out of line with the saturation in Divine Love that has come to him. A mystic like Thomas Traherne asks of his seventeenth-century Anglican Church why, in its Puritan passion, it focusses so exclusively on redemption and why it seems to ignore that redemption is for the purpose of bringing men and women into communion with God, a gift little cultivated in the church of his day. Meister Eckhart's story—of the old woman stalking through the streets of Strasbourg with a pail of water in one hand and a lighted torch in the other, who, when asked what she was doing, replied that with the pail of water she meant to put out the flames of hell and with the lighted torch she meant to burn up heaven so that in the future men might love the Lord God for himself alone and not out of fear of hell or craving for the reward of heaven—is never a favorite anecdote with the religious establishment. Yet here, too, the mystic's witness is not only an attack upon legalism but is a source of continual restoration of focus and a perennial spring of renewal to the religious tradition.

In the matter of religio-cultural values, it has been the mystic who has often broken out of the tribal and provincial bounds and reaffirmed the New Testament ethic of unlimited liability that men bear for their brothers. Francis of Assisi at Acre is believed to have risked his life in order to visit the Sultan, the very symbol of the infidel enemy, and to express to him the unlimited affection which he had for him and his fellow Muslims—and all of this in the midst of the

Christian crusades. The mystics Ramón Lull and Nicholas of Cusa both expressed their passionate concern for the Muslim with a whole new level of understanding in their approach to him that is not even remotely present in the religio-cultural tradition of their time. These are examples of a kind of wider ecumenism that the mystic has brought to bear on traditional religion. The mystic's reopening of the springs of compassion in his day and his gift to the education of the heart in his generation is no small talent, although it has often been misinterpreted by the parochial minds of his time as the Trojan horse of a destructive tolerance and a treasonous inclusiveness.

At the second session of Vatican Council II in Rome it was interesting to see these lines between the mystical and the traditional being drawn over the issue of the Roman Catholic Church's openness to charisms or mystical insights. Cardinal Suenens championed a defining of the Church in such a way that it would be indicated how much the Church cherished these charisms which might be given by God to the simplest members for the sake of the whole. Cardinal Ruffini, a traditionalist leader, would have none of it, implying that these charisms may have flourished in the apostolic period of the Church but that they could be assumed to have been chiefly discontinued at its conclusion, and any appearance of them in the contemporary Church should be viewed with the greatest suspicion!

The levelling, egalitarian aspects of an acknowledgment of such mystical insights that might come to anyone should not be overlooked in any appraisal of what the mystical experience may communicate to the cultural tradition. In a country like India the God-expectancy of the most simple people in the back villages that gives them such a dignity is one of the marks of a culture which has been profoundly affected by the mystical dimension of religion.

The Mystical Experience and "Pointing"

When it comes to the intellectual and philosophical climate that mysticism may help to generate and to the philosophical posture in which it may find itself most at home, there must be great frankness at the outset. Theistic mysticism cannot claim to furnish some infallible occult information on which specific decisions can be made. Nor can it supply some final philosophical or theological formulation of the ultimate questions that might be set down dogmatically in the fashion of a Swedenborg or of some Rosicrucian seer. We must accept William James's suggestion that was mentioned earlier: that the mystical experience opens up a new country but that it does not supply us with a map. We could also add that it does not supply the mystic with a new set of faculties. Almost all the great interpreters have insisted that the mystical experience enters into and heightens the powers of the human faculties that all men and women share.

Yet it would be false to the significance of the mystical experience to stop here. For the mystical pioneer, while not supplied with a map, is encouraged by the experience that the new territory is explorable and that the explorer is a figure worth encouraging.

When a Walt Whitman declares that, "And I know the hand of God is the elder hand of my own," he is witnessing to philosophy not that the dualities, the clefts in experience and knowledge, do not exist, but rather that they are ultimately transcended, and that even if in our own experience, a remainder always exists, the mystic has touched the ground of its overcoming and in one flash has validated both the intellectual seeker and the quest.

It is interesting to note the fearlessness of the mystical educators of the fifteenth century, the Brethren of the Common Life, in whose schools Nicholas of Cusa, Alexander Hegius, and Erasmus were all believed to have been educated. They found no threat but only an enrichment in the new level of classical learning that came with this Northern Spring tide. Firm at the mystical center, they were very free at the periphery. Nicholas of Cusa went even further and welcomed the new physical sciences that were being taught in Italy.

If, as I have assumed to be the case, there would seem to be a dim presence of natural mysticism in all people, the great mystical witness seems to be an articulation and fulfillment of this. This may account for the mystics not only being intelligible to, but even the spokespersons of, a ground of concern in the common man.

At the very moment when the mystic witnesses to the philosophical process that the ground, that the ultimately real is accessible, is all of one piece, and that it invites the quest, it witnesses in the very same breath to the perpetual wraith of cloud, the ultimate mystery, that always surrounds the heights of both the ultimately real and even the ground of the subject that seeks unity with the ultimately real.

This correlative mood does not or should not paralzye the philosophical process of inquiry but only induce a humility about the ultimate reticence of the real and the ultimate reticence of the creative self that seeks the real. The real is not exhaustively portrayed by the conceptual net that is flung over it. Nor is the self that flung out the net in response to the impact of the real exhausted by the projection of this particular net. With the Brahma, it might almost say, "Having created this universe with a part of myself—I remain." The self still has an infinte store of nets with which to follow the present one as it gets a fresh synoptic vision.

This means that no absolutization of any scientific net is ever possible and yet that the provisional significance of any given net and of the very process of projection may be warmly affirmed.

The congeniality of the mystical witness to those who have worked in the area of symbolism is no secret. A symbol "points" (a word precious to Wittgenstein) to the real, but only in its bastardization does it ever claim to *be* the real or to be the only symbol that could be devised to arouse us to an awareness of the real. Dean Inge quoted, on more than one occasion, the line from R. L. Nettleship which says, "True mysticism is the consciousness that everything that we experience is only an element in the fact, i.e. that in being what it is, it is symbolic of more."[38]

Here, again, is the dual role of the mystic, the affirmation and fearlessness toward science and toward the philosophical quest, and at the same time the witness to a plenitude in the ultimately real that makes all of our efforts at plumbing it, even at their best, aware of their provisional character. This devaluation of the transitory, this hint at what Professor Whitehead calls "the fallacy of misplaced concretion" to which all intellectual effort is so vulnerable, is the correlative gift of mysticism to the philosophical process.

Mystical Experience and the Most Congenial Philosophical Posture

As a concluding note to this paper, I should like to look swiftly at four well-known philosophical postures in order to indicate the one in which I think that the mystical phenomena would be most congenial and in which they might contribute most suggestively to the philosophical outlook. Certainly there is no single system of philosophy that could claim any exclusive rights to fulfill these specifications.

Hegel and Schelling have both been deeply moved by mystical phenomena, especially by that found in Meister Eckhart and Jacob Boehme. That mind undergirds all and that it is possible to have direct access to this undergirding reality by an immediate experience seemed highly important data for them. Hegel insisted that it was the philosopher's role to discern the operative formula of the self-manifestation of this ground, and in the course of doing so, he raised the rational process by which this was done into something higher than the immediate experience itself; yet this idealistic interpretation is a possible philosophical setting in which mystical experience can be placed. It is interesting that, since Soren Kierkegaard revolted against this highest priority which was given to reason by Hegel, most orthodox Protestant theologians have tended to identify mysticism with this Hegelian form of philosophical idealism, dubious as any such procedure may be.

Pascal seemed to find in his own mystical experience of being plunged into the burning joy of the divine presence and of overcoming his own inward division, a security that encouraged him to take up skeptical weapons and to cut into ribbons the rational maps of man and his universe to be found in Descartes and in the other classical philosophies of his time. As a mystical existentialist, Pascal used skepticism against rationalism, against scientific materialism, and against all institutional and historical certainty. Existentialism seemed to commend itself to him as a congenial philosophy of arousement to waken men and women out of what he called their "Gethsemane sleep" and to compel them to take a stand, to make a choice about their response to their destiny. The skeptical side of Pascal's philosophical approach toward any certainty but the last has a certain plausibility in it for the mystic and parallels the Negative Theology's attempt to express the plenitude he has been swept by through an attack on lesser modes of expression.

I find it difficult ever to consider existentialism as more than an auxiliary or preparative philosophy, because of its readiness to ignore nature, to pour contempt on all ontology, and to lay its entire focus upon the willed choices of the subject. But in Pascal, where his scientific mastery of the burgeoning physical world of the seventeenth century and his mystical touch with the religious ground that underlay it all are never in question, this auxiliary philosophical position of existentialism seemed to furnish him with a highly effective weapon to bring down the pretensions of both classical philosophy and equally of the newly disclosed infinitely vast universe that science had laid bare, and to sharpen certain inward choices that one stands before in life. Yet Pascal seemed from the security of this mystical experience to have been little troubled by the obviousness of the gaping incompleteness of this philosophy of existentialism.

Roman Catholic thought has wrestled with mystical experience and has believed that it was able to fit it into some form of realism. The Thomistic position itself was not designed primarily to respond to the phenomena of the mystical experience but rather to reconcile the created world of nature with the revealed world of the Bible and of Christian tradition. Yet its view of the beatific vision as the culminating and synoptic gift that would never contradict but only confirm what was given to men and women in both nature and revelation indicates the attempt to include it in their realistic terms. A contemporary Thomist like Jacques Maritain sought to make this final level of mystical disclosure the capstone of his *Degrees of Knowing* and believed that it belongs in that role in any really inclusive realist approach. Because Maritain did this without any basic revision of the Thomistic philosophy of nature or its categories of sense or of abstraction, it has not had, outside of Roman Catholic circles, the attention that it deserves.

Baron Friedrich von Hügel, in his great two-volume edition of *The Mystical Element of Religion,* has wrestled more vigorously than any other Roman Catholic thinker in our century to put the case for the mystical phenomena being more congenially and adequately dealt with in some form of *critical* realism than in any other philosophical stance. His work was completed before the recent existentialist burst had come upon us, but it was carefully enough done and tender enough to the subjective factor in apprehension that it has not been brushed aside by the existentialist insights of our generation. Von Hügel drove his principal case against all forms of idealism as being inadequate to account for the givenness, the otherness, the sheer transcendent aspect of the mystical encounter. Idealism seemed to him to overpress the identity hypothesis in which the self and the Self are assumed to be of the same substance. For him, this wiped out the cleft across which the gift of the mystical experience floods; dissolved away all of the authentic thrust of the givenness of the experience; destroyed the mystery of the overcoming of the cleft; and collapsed the very situation in which prayer and worship and adoration become significant acts.

The realist posture, on the other hand, seemed to von Hügel as adequate not only to describe the inflooding of the mystical experience but the fact that, with the very miracle of communication, there was also an experience of a plenitude that transcended any vessels that the mind had to contain it. Professor Zaehner in his book on Hinduism has seemed to confirm this basic accent of von Hügel when he analyzes the mystical position of the Indian Sankara and finds that it, too, discloses certain hints of theistic mysticism. Zaehner points out that even in the identity-bent Sankara, where the accent is so strongly upon the self's being taught to drop its claim to independent existence and to acknowledge its ground in the cosmic soul as all that there is, that at the very point of this merging, there is reported to be this same sense of impact with the infinite plenitude that literally dwarfs the infinitesimal focus of consciousness that stands before it.

Without in any way invalidating von Hügel's position, we could revise this somewhat exclusively critical-realist approach by introducing an existentialist dimension to deal with the many-dimensioned involvement of the self in any such mystical encounter and have a form of existential realism that has already appeared in fragmentary form in the thought of Gabriel Marcel and that would have much to commend it not only for its large degree of adequacy to the phenomena of mysticism but also to the approach to nature and to the aesthetical and ethical realms to which it is the task of any adequate philosophy to respond.

In all of these closing remarks about the relation of the mystical experience to religion, to ethics, to cultural values, and to philosophy, I am aware that there is a certain betrayal that is present. For the mystical experience does not have to justify itself in terms of its assistance to other areas of life. It has an inherent claim to be good in itself. Tagore says somewhere in his *Reminiscences* in speaking about the experience of ultimate reality, which was not unknown to him, that "if science and philosophy can gain anything from it, they are welcome, but that is not the reason of its being. If while crossing a ferry, you can catch a fish, you are a lucky man, but that does not make the ferry-boat a fishing boat, nor should you abuse the ferry man if he does not making fishing his business." I should like to close by agreeing that Tagore's priorities are the right ones, but that I am nevertheless thankful that the ferrying and the fishing, far from excluding each other, may even be able to illuminate each other.

Notes

1. Pascal, "Everyman," *Thoughts* (New York: Dutton, 1931), no. 283, p. 80.
2. *Meister Eckhart,* ed. F. Pfeiffer, trans. C. de B. Evans (London: Watkins, 1924), p. 255.
3. Bernard of Clairvaux, *Sermons on Canticles,* 74 (5,6).
4. Jan Ruysbroeck, *The Adornment of the Spiritual Marriage,* trans. C. A. W. Dom (London: Dent, 1916), p. 131.
5. *Meister Eckhart,* p. 231.
6. Ibid., p. 240.
7. Ibid., p. 237.
8. Ibid., p. 45.
9. St. John of the Cross, *Works,* trans. Allison Peers (Westminster, Maryland: New Man, 1946), III:15.
10. Ibid., pp. 20–21.
11. Ibid., I:439.
12. Ibid., III:28.
13. Ibid., pp. 39, 32.
14. Friedrich von Hügel, *The Mystical Element of Religion* (London: Dent, 1908), I:105–125.
15. George Fox, *Journal* (New York: Dutton, 1948), p. 35.
16. Jan Ruysbroeck, p. 74.
17. Ibid., p. 87.
18. G. Santayana, *The Life of Reason: Reason in Religion* (London: Constable, 1905), pp. 29, 278–9.
19. John Woolman, *Journal,* Whittier Edition (New York: Houghton Mifflin, 1871), pp. 58–9.
20. E. I. Watkin, *Philosophy of Mysticism* (London: Richards, 1920), p. 133.
21. F. Max Planck, *The Philosophy of Physics,* trans. W. H. Johnston (New York: W. W. Norton, 1936), pp. 121 ff.

22. William James, *Varieties of Mystical Experience* (New York: Longmans, 1928), p. 388.
23. Teresa of Avila, *Works,* trans. Allison Peers (London: Sheed and Ward, 1944), I:105.
24. Meister Eckhart, p. 281.
25. Ibid., p. 13.
26. Jan Ruysbroeck, p. 44.
27. Ibid., p. 88.
28. Manuscript copy.
29. William Ernest Hocking, *Types of Philosophy* (New York: Scribner's, 1928), p. 455.
30. Ibid., p. 392.
31. E. I. Watkin, pp. 60–61.
32. John of the Cross, I:82.
33. Ibid., III:107.
34. Robert Barclay, *Apology,* Prop. 11, Section VII.
35. Teresa of Avila, *Works,* I:182; ct. 111, 162.
36. J. B. Pratt, *Religious Consciousness* (New York: Macmillan, 1920), p. 463.
37. Von Hügel, II:29, 31–32.
38. W. R. Inge, *Mysticism in Religion* (Chicago: University of Chicago Press, 1948), p. 44.

On Being Present
Where You Are*

T he word *presence* has taken on a new assignment in our generation. We have come to speak of the United Nations *presence* in Lebanon or the Quaker *presence* in Delhi or in Geneva. We assume that it means that the UN or the Quakers are *there*. We assume also, though this may be a gross exaggeration, that this presence is felt and ac- knowledged by those whom it touches, and that it is making a differ- ence—we hope a favorable difference—to the situation. But are these assumptions correct? Is presence possible when there is almost no physical representative on the scene? It has often seemed to me that slave-tortured Africa was more acutely present to Scotland and to Britain in David Livingstone's day over a century ago, when there were only a handful of widely scattered missionaries and consuls about, than Africa today, when tens of thousands of British citizens are actively at work on this continent. What, then, does it mean to be present and what does genuine presence imply?

If we return to our own childhood, do you recall sitting in a class- room as a child while the teacher took the roll? When your name was called out, you answered "present." You might have been half asleep, or had your mind on what part of the stream you were going to fish on the next day, which was Saturday, or be worrying about whether the teacher would call on you to put your solution of the arithmetic problem on the board, but you still mustered up enough response to register that you were *present*.

* First published as Pendle Hill Pamphlet 151 © 1967 by Pendle Hill, Quaker Study Center at Wallingford, Pennsylvania 19086. Used with permission.

What does it really mean to be present in any given place or at any given time? Certainly when I answered the roll call, all that the teacher was recording was my physical presence: Douglas Steere's body is seated at this school desk today. But the teacher assumed more than that when she heard my answer, "present." Rightly or wrongly, she assumed that not only my body was present but that my mind was available for the day's workout, and that she could communicate with my mind, perhaps even influence it, if she chose to put a question to me, and perhaps if I was elsewhere or especially stubborn and preoccupied, she could stimulate my mind a little by the application of a light nip from her willow pointer to call me back to attention. I must confess that my answer of "present" on many school days did not live up to the teacher's assumptions.

Do you recall at the age of say, twelve, how some person of the opposite sex of whom you had been almost completely oblivious, suddenly stepped up out of the blur and became intensely present to you? Do you remember how, in a cluster of adult relatives of whom you were dimly aware, one or two of them were vividly present to you?

One time a friend of ours told us of entertaining her six-year-old daughter's friends at a birthday party and of how she tried to enter into the fun in kittenish ways as if she too were a little girl. As one of the children was leaving, the hostess said to her, "I'll bet you think Carol's mummy is a very funny old person," and received the reply, "I don't think about you at all!" She had not been even remotely present to this little girl during the whole party.

There were, however, a few adults whom you *did* think about and they mattered terribly to you. I recall two aunts who were ever so present to me. Within a single month one left for a long sojourn in the Philippine Islands as a teacher and the other went off with her husband to live on the other side of our continent, and I was utterly desolate and bereft. My brother and sister and parents were still there, but I took them for granted and they were largely a part of the household furniture at that stage and nothing like so present to me as these aunts had been. Then I came down with scarlet fever and after a month in a public contagious hospital, I was released too soon and my seven-year-old sister caught the disease and died. Suddenly in her absence she was present as she had rarely been in her active life, and for many months after this my sister Helen lived closer to me than ever in life. She was no longer physically present and yet she was present in a thousand ways: in love, in remorse, in loneliness, in wistfulness, until life closed over this presence and it became only an occasional and yet a very precious one. The fact that a departed one could be more present in her physical absence than in her living contact was a strange discovery for a twelve-year-old boy and one with some searching implications for the life beyond this life that I cannot develop here. Later it was to help me to understand Jesus' saying that it might be better for him to go away and to come to them from within as an inward comforter.

Another experience of presence which came in my childhood dug the dimension deeper. I read a life of Abraham Lincoln, and Lincoln, to whose family a forbear of my father's belonged, stalked out of the oblivion of fifty years of death and became a hero and almost a companion of mine. He was present for me—far more present than many people whom I was able to see and to touch and to talk with every day. T. S. Eliot points out how often we find our true contemporaries not in our own generation, but they walk out of other ages and lay hold of us, are acutely present to us, and we know them for our own. He confesses that Lancelot Andrewes, the seventeenth-century Anglican whose *Private Devotions* are familiar to many of you, was vividly present as such a living contemporary to him.

We may prepare ourselves for this broadening of the notion of presence by recalling how many times in our lives we have felt the vivid presence of another when he or she was thousands of miles away, felt it far more acutely than when we could actually reach out and touch that individual in the very same room. To be *present,* then, can on one level mean to be locatable at a given point in space and time. But two persons (even two married persons) or two races or two religions or two cultures can live in precisely the same place and at the very same moment of time and yet can brush past each other with no more understanding of each other or effect upon each other than what Dr. Jacques Cuttat calls "a dialogue of deafs."

Bergson, Grisebach, and Kant on the One Who Is Present

For a person or a cluster of persons to be locatable in a given space and time is a *kind* of being present to each other—but it is a far cry from exhausting what real presence means. Henri Bergson, in his *Creative Evolution,* speaks of "a body as present wherever its (attractive) influence is felt" (p. 198). This is a highly suggestive definition and might go far to light up some of the instances suggested above. It seems on the surface to contrast sharply with that of the German theologian, Eberhard Grisebach, whose word for presence, *Gegenwart,* literally means "that which waits over against me." In other words, presence is that in the other which resists me, which I cannot manipulate; that which I confront.

If the relationship of persons is what is being referred to, it is conceivable that these two conceptions of presence are not really in conflict but may turn out to be truly complementary to each other. For Bergson's dynamic definition of presence in terms of influence or penetration or power to transform, and Grisebach's more static concept of presence in terms of a resistance which tends to elicit my acknowledgment of it, may each disclose an aspect of encounter. Neither dares be absent if the being present to each other is to penetrate to the deeper dimensions.

As a matter of fact, I believe Immanuel Kant in his second formulation of the categorical imperative (the built-in sense of duty in us all) is making the same reservation that Grisebach is making. "Treat humanity, whether in yourself or in others, always as an end and never as a means." If presence meant only the Bergsonian operative influence which one person might have upon another, this influence might well be exploitive or destructive. For there is in all of us an inclination to order our environment, including its human members, from our own axis outwards. Grisebach, like Kant, would therefore accent the integrity of a fellow subject, the waiting resistance, the overagainstness, the incorruptible integrity in the other that is open to influence but that also operates from a mysterious and highly important axis of its own.

In the matter of persons, then, if we were to attempt to characterize this further dimension of presence that goes beyond locatability, we should have to speak of its posture as a readiness to respect and to stand in wonder and openness before the mysterious life and influence of the other. It means, to be sure, a power to influence, to penetrate, to engage with the other; but it means equally a willingness to be vulnerable enough to be influenced by, to be penetrated by, and even to be changed by the experience. If this is an accurate account of what actually takes place on the deepest levels of love and of friendship, it also means that out of the long loneliness of life there are possible some luminous moments of profound communion, of truly coming into the presence of the other. And when they do come, all efforts to measure their worth seem superfluous.

Presence and Four Types of Love

An essay by the Spanish existentialist philosopher, Ortega y Gasset, speaks about the different kinds of love that may exist between a man and a woman. He describes first of all the physical love in which one or both of the partners wants to use the other as a source of physical gratification and the whole relationship is contrived in order to maximize this possibility. The partner is "used," quite possibly most willingly used, to give the other the gratification that he seeks, but he or she is present to the other only as a thing, an object and condition of that self-gratification.

He then describes a second type of love that is much more perverse than the first type. It is a love that has as its goal the psychological conquest of the other partner. When the partner can be induced to fall in love and to submit and to be dominated, then the operation is complete and the interest in the presence of the other wanes. He or she becomes just one more mounted trophy in the game-room of the mind. "When the fish is in the boat the fun is all over."

A third type of love may involve the two partners in each projecting an image upon the other; an image of what the loved object should be like. It may be an image that has come from their own father or mother or from some dream idyll. Having projected this image upon the partner, they then proceed to focus their love upon the image. The image may have little or no relationship to the real person of the other; in fact it may even threaten to strangle, to smother, and even to destroy the true life of the partner quite as much as the great serpents threaten the lives of the figures in the Greek sculpture, the Laocoön, and each may be struggling as fiercely as these Greek victims in order to try to extricate himself. In many instances, the struggle for integrity fails and the projected image prevails, and when this happens, neither can be present to the other except in this disguise.

In the fourth type of love, which Ortega only hints at, something of Rilke's brilliant flash of insight enters when he describes love as "two solitudes" that "protect and touch and greet each other." Each is willing to drop, or at least to lower, the projected image and to feel an increasing sense of responsibility that the other should fulfill the mysterious destiny that God has hidden within him or her, whether this shatters the image or not. Each counts it an infinite blessing to be able to live in the presence of the other and to be forever surprised by the joy of seeing the other grow from the deepest inner vision that is hidden in him or her.

Sometimes the loved one himself loses the vision and the one who loves him is prepared to suffer, sustain, and to have faith in him during the time that he is in flight from his destiny. Often enough there are storms and crises and it is only in the moments of forgiveness and reconciliation that this fourth type of relationship emerges or is restored. There can be little doubt that the postcrisis presence is often superior to the precrisis one for it has been tested and has been vindicated. Sometimes it is only when the partner has been threatened with some form of extinction that the reverence for the mystery and wonder of the true person in the partner surfaces, and for the first time the real person is present to the partner.

This fourth level searches each of us to the quick not only in our friendships and marriage but also in our contacts with other religions, races, and nations. We long to be truly present to each other, but we tremble before the possible cost of such vulnerability and are tempted to settle for something less exacting.

On Being "All There"

People sometimes speak of a person suffering from a mental disease as being not "all there." It is a strange expression, but a telling one, for true sanity might well be defined negatively as the absence of elsewhereness, or positively as the quality of being fully present to any situation into which I may be drawn. I am sane when I am *all there*.

How searching this *being there* in situations of need really is! Tolstoy, in his famous *Twenty-three Tales,* devotes the final one to describing a king who is in search of an answer to three questions: How can I learn to do the right thing at the right time? Whose advice can

I trust? And what things are most important and require my first attention?

Disguised in simple clothes, the king visited a hermit deep in the wood and asked him his three questions. Getting no answer but finding the frail hermit on the verge of collapse, the king took over the hermit's spade and finished digging his garden. At sunset a bearded man staggered in with a terrible bleeding stomach wound, dealt him by one of the king's bodyguards who were scattered through the forest to protect him. The king washed the wound, bandaged it with a towel and handkerchief, and kept changing the bandages until the flow of blood stopped and the man could be carried into the hut. The king slept the night on the threshold of the hut and when morning came, found the bearded man confessing that he had lain in wait for the king's return from the hermit's hut, having sworn to kill him for a judgment the king had once given against him. He begged the king's forgiveness and pledged to serve him. The king, promising to send his own physician to attend him, rose to go but again put his questions to the hermit, complaining that he had still received no answer to them.

The hermit insisted that the king had twice received his answers on the previous day: When the king appeared on the previous afternoon, the hermit in his weakness did not see how he could finish digging his garden, and the king had relieved him. This was the right thing at the right time and the most important to be done—for had he returned through the wood at that time, his enemy would have killed him. When the wounded man appeared, stanching his blood and relieving him was the right thing at the right time and made a friend of an enemy. "Remember then," added the hermit, "there is only one time that is important. Now!" And, further, "The most necessary man is he with whom you are . . . and the most important thing is to do him good, because for that purpose alone was man sent into this life!"

But to qualify for making anything of this bone-bare answer of the hermit's, of our being present where immediate need is to be found, you have to be *all* there. You have to be awake. You cannot be in a drowse of preoccupation, in what Pascal called the *Gethsemane-sleep,* where Jesus' disciples failed him three times by drowsing off, by not being present where they were.

There is a moving scene in Augustine's *Confessions* where Augustine seems ripe for the spiritual turning, for the big change, and where the one man he longed to speak with was Bishop Ambrose. Again and again Augustine walked hopefully past the open door of the Cathedral library where Ambrose was sitting absorbed in his reading. Ambrose was present for Augustine, but Augustine was not present for Ambrose. Knowing how busy Ambrose was, Augustine could not muster the courage to disturb him, so he went away and his conversation was further delayed.

Martin Buber, in his *Between Man and Man,* tells of a student who came to him for counsel. Buber listened to his story and gave him professionally competent advice, and the student went away and took his own life. Buber goes on to tell how he was searched to the core of his being as to whether if he had been really present, really engaged, really all there for that student, the outcome would have been the same.

The Cost of Being Present

But to be really present to another requires even more than all-thereness. There was an old piece of advice among the early Franciscan Third Order of lay Christians that the giving of alms, the equivalent of our "checkbook charity," was not enough. The members of the Third Order were to seek to find ways in which they could mix their bodies, their personal service, with their alms. Francis' own spontaneous acts gave them the clue when he kissed the blind man's face into whose hands he pressed assistance, or when at the leper hutch at Rivo Torto he not only brought food but dressed the leper's sore. The members were to be personally present where they helped, and always to search for fresh ways to show that they cared and were mixed with the victim's situation. The small-town gifts of food and offers of service that tumble in with such profusion when heavy sickness or death stalks a neighbor's household often have about them much of this Franciscan flavor. To be personally present in what you do gives some earnest that you mean it.

When, in the Old Testament story, the Shunamite woman whose son is stricken hastens to the mountains, hunts out and finds the prophet Elisha, and gets his instant promise to come and minister to her son, Elisha's first act is to send his servant companion on ahead of him with instructions to lay his staff on the boy's body. But this produces no effect. On his own arrival, Elisha kneels before the bed on which the stricken boy is lying and prays to God to restore to life this only son of these devout parents, but still there is no change. In this moving story, it is only when Elisha lays his own body over the body of the boy and breathes his own breath into the boy's nostrils, that the boy returns to consciousness and is restored to his family. To be really present may be at no less cost of involvement.

A Real Friend Is Present

When it comes to our friendships, how shallow these often seem to be, and how seldom are we really present to a friend! Is it that this cost of presence is so high that we shrink from more than soft outside friendships? A member of our Quaker Meeting was suffering from an acute diabetic condition that had brought her not only blindness but the prospect that at most she had only a year or two to live. In response to the Meeting's query about members who wished to visit her, she sent word that she did not want visits from anyone who meant to come only once or twice. She did not need to be diverted by courtesy calls. Her life was now too short for making acquaintances unless they really meant it. "Please don't come unless you mean to continue to come."

These terms of hers point toward the cost of presence. For really to be present to another, to be a true friend, means to be forever on call, forever open, forever willing to be involved in the friend's troubles as well as his or her joys. Pierre Ceresole, the beloved Swiss Quaker pioneer and founder of the International Work Camps, once wrote in his private journal, "The moment, the critical moment where true friendship or true love begins, is when one feels that if he or she has really done something grievous and regrettable or even criminal— well it is exactly as if one had done it oneself."

One of the vital ad hoc churches in the Christian world today, where men and women are really present to each other, is in Alcoholics Anonymous, where the one agreeing to link his or her life with yours is ready to come to you anywhere, at any hour of the day and night, and on no notice at all in order to meet your need—and both of you know in advance that there will be need.

In the writing of a letter, the epistle can be a kind of hurried calendar of events with a formal solicitous inquiry about your condition at its conclusion, and it will be quite clear to the receiver that as it was being written he was hardly present at all to the writer. Or the letter can be written in such a way that the receiver knows instinctively that he and his situation are present to the writer throughout. I was touched in the summer of 1965 to get a letter from Albert Schweitzer in reply to one I had written him just after his ninetieth birthday. In the course of telling me about his life in Lambarené, he asked me if I did not miss giving my college lectures now that I was retired. With the hundreds of things he had to do, he had been concerned truly to enter into my life and situation.

A real friend is present. He is there when you need him. A real friend seems to know the word to speak, or the question to ask, or the book to send in order to help to restore for us the lost image of our life task. He knows how to confirm in us the deepest thing that is already there, "answering to that of God" in his needy friend.

In offering hospitality, the outer side, the comforts, the diversions the host provides may exhaust what he has to give and the visit may pass without host or guest ever being really present to each other. Or the occasion of hospitality may be a time where the host and guest have not only some leisure for each other but they become truly present to each other and whether through a press of the hand, or in talk, or in silence, or in a walk, or in the things they do for each other, something opens in them both and something happens. The visits of Jesus to Bethany must have been like that. He and his hostesses, Mary and Martha, to say nothing of Lazarus, must have been present to each other.

I had a visit not long ago from an old friend in whose Scandinavian home I once enjoyed all of the graces of true hospitality and I recall vividly his word with me an hour before my departure about what he felt I had been given to do in this swiftly passing life. No other person can ever chart a course for you, but a friend and a host who is really present can at times firm up what you in your own deepest heart of hearts have already felt drawing at you. And he did just this for me, and in that moment we both knew that we were truly present to each other.

The family-visiting of Quakers travelling in the ministry must have had some of this same note about it. The visiting Friend sought to be truly open and present to members of the family as he visited with each one about the spiritual condition of his life at that time.

"I Am Ready, Are You Ready?"

Presence may also come in an act of prayer. For in the life of prayer we bring ourselves into an openness that makes it possible for us to be freshly aware of God's presence. It is not that he is not present at other times but that by this voluntary act of ours, the act of prayer, we are enabled to break with our outer preoccupations and to become aware of the presence and of what that presence does to search and to transform and to renew us and to send us back into life again.

A speaker was once introduced by the perfect chairman who said simply, "Mr. Weaver, we are ready. Are you ready?" When I gather myself for prayer it is almost as if God were so addressing me: "Douglas Steere, I am ready. Are you ready?" And my answer is, "O Lord, you are always ready but am I ever ready? O Lord, make me ready, or at least make me more ready to be made ready."

In prayer where intercession is involved, I make those for whom I am praying present for myself by thinking of them and of their need and of the One who can meet that need in its deepest sense. Perhaps my friend is swept by a persistent temptation to which he has yielded often enough to threaten to glaze over his life, to numb the heart core in him, and finally to cut him off from ever sensing the deepest spring of love in another person or in the One that sustains him with both an unceasing and an unspeakable love. In my prayer I make him present to me by thinking intensively of him and of the threshold over which both God's and my own caring must pass in order to reach him. I think, too, of this whole solace of intercessory caring which God's love and the love of the whole communion of saints is forever drawing at his life. My own caring for him is frail in comparison to this, but I feel that it is swept up into this greater net of attracting energy and that for all of its frailty it may be the decisive impulse that may touch my friend's decision and open him to these ever present forces that could change his whole perspective.

In intercessory prayer my friend may be more truly present to me than as if I were literally never out of his sight. I believe that this is why Forbes Robinson could say in all sincerity that he would rather have half an hour of prayer *for* his friend than hours of conversation *with* him. The friend, and the provident mercy of God and his redemptive company, might well be far more present to him in the one situation than in the other, although intercessory prayer and conversation are far from mutually exclusive. In a conversation itself I may be in intense intercession.

In intercessory prayer, however, where I and my friend may be acutely present to each other and to the ground of infinite compassionate love, it is not only my friend who is irradiated and opened to transformation but my own life as well, for two persons can never be truly present to each other or to the living God and remain the same. When E. Herman says, "To come near to God is to change," she might as readily have said, "To be present to God, either alone or in the presence of another, is to change," for to be present is to be open to influence.

The Unbidden Presence

Prayer is a voluntary means that is given as an ever available door by which to come into God's presence. But his presence often enough comes to us unbidden and overwhelms us when we least expect it and we have only our usual abysmal need to attract it. Hugh Walpole tells of a day in the First World War when he held a horribly wounded Austrian soldier in his arms for half an hour as he slipped out of this life. He felt the presence in that man as never before. Charles Raven, in his autobiography, *A Wanderer's Way,* speaks of how in Liverpool "on my walks in the mean streets, God met me in splendour. Always the sense of His presence was unexpected, even startling in the suddenness of the manifestation. . . . I was coming home after a long tramp and passed some shawl-clad women gathered round a dingy shop. The proprietor, in his shirt sleeves, was dispensing packets of fish and chips wrapped in a newspaper. The place was lit by naphtha flares, and misty with the steam of cooking. . . . And again of a sudden the glory; and God fulfilling his eternal task and giving to his children their daily bread." (New York: Henry Holt, 1929, p. 109, 11.) Brother Lawrence was overcome by the Lord's presence as he gazed at a tree.

Who of us does not quicken to the lines in Wordsworth's Tintern

Abbey, "And I have felt a presence that disturbs me with the joy of elevated thoughts"? Who of us has no notion of what Evelyn Underhill means by speaking of the inward "slowing down" or what George Fox means when he speaks of God's "turning of the wheel of his life within us"? Who has never felt melted down and brought to tears of tenderness at a great passage in a book, a scene in a play, a sight of the sea, a word or the hug of a child, a surge of pain, a midnight hour in a "white night" when we have been shown the way and have yielded, or at one of those moments in a conversation with a friend where we touched "where words come from"? These minor ecstasies, as Elizabeth Vining calls them, are all fingers. They all point to the presence. William Blake knowingly says, "There is a moment in each day which Satan cannot find," and at these moments it is as if we heard again, "I am ready. Are you ready? I am present. Are you present?" And now and then we dare to whisper the answer, "I am present, Lord. I am present where I am, and you are present with me."

The "Dialogue of Deafs" Among the World Religions

In contemporary Japan the indigenous Christian churches have been living for well over a century in the midst of a Buddhist society, and in India, for many centuries imbedded in a Hindu society, as though these fellow world religions did not exist, as though they simply were not present.

The Swiss orientalist, Dr. Jacques Cuttat, states, "Up to the end of the 19th century, the monotheistic Jewish, Christian, Moslem communities of India lived side by side with Hindus and Buddhists, tolerated by them but also spiritually unrelated with them." (*The Spiritual Dialogue: East and West,* p. 38.)

The problem today is "What does it mean to be present where we are?" For centuries many Christians in these countries have not been present where they were. They have despised and looked down upon the reigning world religions that they or their forbears left and have simply shunned them. In doing this they have often shunned a deep part of their own hidden life.

The fact that after all of these years of the most intensive missionary effort, perhaps one-half of one percent of the Japanese people and two and one-half percent of the Indian population have become Christians would seem to be saying something to us. But an even more serious concern might be found in the fact that in India, Indian Christians have learned almost nothing from this long exposure of the Indian Christian church to one of the greatest spiritual vehicles of the world —to Hinduism. The result is that Indian Christians, with a few exceptions like Sadhu Sundar Singh, have rarely brought into the world's Christian treasury anything really unique or distinctive. In their worship, theology, devotional practice, and Christian social mutations, they have tended to exemplify a non-Asiatic version of institutionalized Western Christianity. A Black friend of mine once asked Gandhi what was the greatest handicap that Jesus had in India, and instantly Gandhi replied, "Christianity."

The problem that imaginative Indian Christian leaders confess they face is how to awaken the Indian Christian to discover what it means to be present where he is, and to come into vital and life-affecting contact with his Hindu brother and sister and with his Indian heritage. Only as he overcomes his fear and dares to do this is he likely to have a fresh gift to offer on the altar of the world. To engage in this contact does not mean to weaken his new-found Christian faith. Nor does it mean that if he acknowledges Hinduism or Buddhism or Islam or any of the great world religious faiths as an important response to the Divine initiative, he has thereby admitted that all religions are equally adequate responses to the Divine Love. It does mean that he stops shunning, stops derision, and begins actively to be present to the creative discoveries that his brother's religion does contain and to the Divine initiative that has never left any people of the world outside its drawing power.

"No Religion Is An Island"

In the United States there are more Jews than in Israel, and their religion has almost from the beginning of our history been something apart, something to which we paid little attention, something that might keep a Jew from attending his shop or coming to a meeting on Saturday, but very little else. They gave us the Old Testament, yes, but why did they fixate at that point? In our day men like Abraham Heschel and Martin Buber have enriched the spiritual life of our Christian people immeasurably by sharing with us some of the great treasures of Judaism. A well-known Jewish columnist, the late Harry Golden, was bold enough to joke with his Christian brothers who once invited him to give a commencement address at a Presbyterian college in North Carolina. Referring to our "God Is Dead" theology in America, Harry Golden assured his Presbyterian friends that they could rest easy, for the Jews would see to it that God was worshipped during this blitz of Protestant theology and that when it was over, the Jews would return God to them to worship again!

Late in his life, Abraham Heschel, in an important address at Union Theological Seminary, dared to speak with great frankness about our deep dependence on each other as adherents of the great religions in this period in which we are living:

> Our era marks the end of complacency, the end of evasion, the end of self-reliance. Jews and Christians share the perils and the fears; we stand on the brink of the abyss together. Interdependence of political and economic conditions all over the world is a basic fact of our situation. Disorder in a small and obscure country in any part of the world evokes anxiety in people all over the world.
>
> The religions of the world are no more self-sufficient, no more independent, no more isolated than individuals or nations; energies, experiences and ideas that come to life outside the boundaries of a particular religion or all religions continue to challenge and affect every religion. No religion is an island. We are all involved with one another. Spiritual betrayal on the part of one of us affects the faith of all of us. . . . Today, religious isolation is a myth.
>
> We must choose between inter-faith and inter-nihilism. Should religions insist upon the illusion of complete isolation? Should we refuse to be on speaking terms with one another and hope for each other's failure?" (*Union Seminary Quarterly Review.* Vol. XXL, no. 2, Part I, Jan. 1966, pp. 119–130.)

I have earlier given an example of a single experience in a Japanese colloquium of a dialogue in depth. But we need far more experiments of all species in order to explore the full thrust of being present to each other. Yet we are not without clues. I have found no one who has helped to formulate the tone and spirit of such meetings more helpfully than the late Jacques Cuttat. He suggests that if those who gather for such an occasion could be brought to have Saint Exupéry's faith that "If I differ from you, far from harming you, I increase you," they might be willing to be present to each other and listen to each other with a new openness.

Cuttat begs us all to learn how to "give to the faith of another the amplitude of love. We must learn how to create an inter-religious space and in such a space, God's spirit can blow as it wills." He believes, as I believe, that the Holy Spirit does have something urgent to say to our highly institutionalized and Westernized Christianity through Hinduism: through its God expectancy, through its belief in simplicity of life, through its continuing practice of inward medita- tion, through its passion for sanctity, and through its sense of thank- fulness that it manifests in so many touching ways.

Presence and the Revolution in Higher Education

If we move from the ecumenical field to that of the process of higher education itself, we in the United States are involved in an educational upheaval that some of us believe may have profound implications for the educational process of the future and that bears directly on the whole issue of the "presence" of the faculty and students to each other. A president of the University of Missouri, Dr. John Weaver, received a copy of a memorandum that had come to him indirectly from the vice president of a college of medicine in a state institution. In part it read: "There is no merit to be gained in teaching; you are expected to bring in twenty to fifty percent of your salary through (research) grants; if you are unwilling to do your share to make this institution internationally famous through research, you are invited to leave." In contrast, John Weaver produced a memo from the chairman of the huge Ohio State mathematics department who, in the course of a curriculum argument, insisted, "Please remember, gentle- men, in my department we aren't working with numbers, we are working with people."

It is the preponderance of vice presidents for the medical sciences and the scarcity of mathematics chairmen of this character that have done much toward alienating students. The students have not felt that they were "present" to the preoccupied faculty; that they were being treated as "people," as mysterious persons with a destiny of their own; and the ways of drawing attention to their situation are often bizarre. I heard from a friend in the Danforth Foundation of a student body in a small Midwestern denominational college who, rebellious at the dull and unreal required chapel programs, instituted a "worship down." They went to chapel as required but they did not rise when the chaplain bid them to do so, and when they did stand up, they remained standing when they were asked to sit down. They had the President and the Dean and the Chaplain over the ropes before they had finished.

Is it possible that the students are saying in these gestures that the time has come when they be regarded as a fourth estate with Faculty and Administration and Boards of Trustees, and that they be given an active voice in the devising of this educational experience of theirs? I believe they are saying that they want to be present to the faculty and administration and to the community in which they live and that they want to have the actual reciprocal response that such presence calls for. I can conceive that the kind of college in the 1980s that may emerge and that we could or should now begin to pioneer might have some of the traits of a reconstituted All Souls College where faculty and students could be jointly engaged in digging out fresh problems and their solutions and where there are no longer faculties and students, but only junior and senior "fellows." This kind of situation where presence to each other would be central in the higher educational process may be closer to us than we are prepared to acknowledge.

Presence and Racial Barriers

When it comes to the whole issue of civil rights and of the place of minority communities inside the larger community, there is a story that has come out of the Blacks' struggle in the United States that shows in a delicious way how strange we white people may look through the opposite end of the telescope. A Black woman who was almost blind and had a seeing-eye dog to guide her got on a bus driven by a white man. She fumbled in getting her change into the fare box and it slipped to the floor. The white driver cursed her, told her to pick it up and put it in the box, and as he made a move toward her, the dog sank his teeth into his leg and then jumped out of the bus and bit the leg of a Black man who was standing on the curb. Talking of the incident afterwards, a neighbor asked the blind woman how she accounted for the fact that her dog who had quite rightly bitten the ugly white bus driver, should jump out and bite the innocent Black man on the curb. The blind woman replied, "I don't know why he did it, unless he just wanted to get that awful taste out of his mouth."

In no area of our time is this issue of presence to be seen more clearly in the United States than in our life with our Black fellow citizens. It is obvious what segregation, and the network of laws and customs that went with it, have done to keep the Blacks from being present to the whites. But in order to try to cover up the hurt, there has also been the less noticed absence of the whites being present to the Blacks. The late Howard Thurman, a Black spiritual leader who is well known to the Christian community in the United States, writes in *The Luminous Darkness,* "When I was a boy growing up in Florida . . . white persons . . . were not read out of the human race—they simply did not belong to it in the first place. Behavior toward them was amoral. They were not hated particularly; they were not essentially despised; they were simply out of bounds. It is very difficult to put into words what was at work here. They were tolerated as a vital part of the environment, but they did not count IN. They were in a world apart, in another universe of discourse." (Harper and Row, New York, 1965, p. 3). How clearly he could have said, *they were not present to each other.*

American liberals have been nursing their wounds in the last few years. They have championed Black freedom vigorously; they have cried out against the officially rejected but doggedly persistent caste system in India that excludes certain occupations from contact with the rest of the community; they have supported SWAPO in its attempts to free Namibia; they favor an ultimate blockade of South Africa for her failure to permit just political representation and freedom of movement to her Black populations. But to his consternation and often his bitter resentment, the American liberal is discovering that in the eyes of his Black brother and sister all of his bold backing of the Black cause has not led to his being either venerated or trusted by Blacks. The unconscious interior colonialism of the heart and the viscera that had led to condescension, to patronizing, to the invisible walls that now at last our Black writers are blistering us by describing; all these point to what makes Blacks want to go it alone, to provide their own leadership, and to writhe out of the embrace of this third type of love where liberal whites focus their sentimental image upon them and proceed to approve them and to lavish favors upon them as long as they stay within their boundaries. These are all across-the-board demands either to be present to the Black person as he is and to penetrate and be penetrated by him, to transform and be transformed by him; or to receive his declaration of war until we can accept him on that basis.

In Interior Emigration

In the personal, ecumenical, educational, and racial areas, to be present, really present, is to be vulnerable, to be able to be hurt. And when pain is in prospect, it is so much easier to be elsewhere than where we are. Pastor Hamel in the German Democratic Republic used to chide his Protestant brothers and sisters who had been made out to be the heroes of Christian Europe by their faithfulness to the suffering church under Communism. He tells them in a striking little book, *The Christian in the DDR,* that far from being Christian heroes, they are nearly all guilty of interior emigration, they live on in the DDR but in nearly every other sense they have already defected to the West. They expect the West ultimately to bail them out either diplomatically or by force, and in their thoughts they already reside in the West, although their bodies are still in the DDR. Hamel goes on to point out that they can never be really present to their Communist brothers and sisters, never be able to influence them, never be able to make even the ghost of a Christian witness to their Communist fellow country-men until they inwardly return to the DDR, are willing to trust the power of God to sustain them there, and are willing to live there, if need be, even until they die. He was bidding them to be present where they are or to give up completely any hope of either effective dialogue or of Christian witness to the Communist neighbor.

How much interior emigration there is all about us! Students emi-grate to the future and are not present where they are. Displaced persons live in the past and refuse to let go to the new homeland and to live where they are. Parents are not present here and now but are living for the day when the children are raised, or when they will retire, or when they will be free of this or that, but remain numb and glazed and absent from the living moment. To be present is to be vulnerable, to be able to be hurt, to be willing to be spent—but it is also to be awake, alive, and engaged actively in the immediate assignment that has been laid upon us.

I believe that in the period that lies ahead, there is no deeper challenge in our personal, spiritual, and social witness all over the globe than this issue of learning to be present where we are in our personal relationships and making our witness and effort to rouse men and women to dare to be present to each other. The issue of peace and war, the issue of racial tensions, the issue of an educational breakthrough, the issue of our responsibility to contribute to the quickening of the relationships of the great world religions—all come down in the end to this daring to be present where we are.

There is One who, on that road out of Jerusalem to the little town of Emmaus, taught his companions of the road and of the table what it was to be present. "Did not our hearts burn within us while he talked with us by the way?" That same quickening presence still walks by our side. That same presence kindles our meetings for worship and reveals to us our failure to be truly present with our families, our friends, and our brothers in the world. It is there in his presence when we are again given the gift of tears, that we are once more joined to all the living, that hope is restored in us, and that we are rebaptized into the sacredness of the gift of life and of the gift of being set down here among fellow humans who, in the depth of their being, long to be truly present to each other. Not only is there "no time but this present," but there is no task God has called us to that is more exciting and challenging than being made inwardly ready to be present where we are.

CONCLUSION

Spiritual Renewal in Our Time

> Sure, holiness the magnet is!
> And love the lure that woos thee down;
> Which makes the high transcendent bliss
> Of knowing thee, so rarely known.
>
> Henry Vaughan

What are we about? We hope in our hearts that we may help to renew the church. But how and where are the clues for the renewal of both ourselves and the church? They are exactly where they always have been, not downstream among vast levies and deltas of programs and plans and administrative structures, but far upstream where all religious renewal comes from: in the quiet places of the hearts of men, in the solitary conversations of consecrated and consecratable souls confronting the mighty acts of God that, by the way, are still going on.

When the young Francis, with the noose of God already drawing tight upon him, knelt before the life-sized crucifix in the little tumble-down chapel of St. Damien in Assisi and received the decisive summons "Renew my church," one of those upstream moments occurred. But it required further clarification for Francis before he discovered what the summons meant. Taking it literally at the outset and begging, buying, borrowing stones and timbers, he went to work to restore the badly decayed chapel itself. He saw before long that something far more costly was being asked of him. Only when the interior life of the church was touched could it ever be renewed, and for that nothing less than a great flood of prayer—nights on end of the slopes of Mt. Subasio, together with the final agony at La Verna—was

179

required to unleash the flood of compassion, of charity, of Christian abandon that such an operation demanded.

When three and a half centuries later an indulgent cloistered Carmelite nun, Teresa of Avila, housed in a Spanish church that had fallen foul of both laxity and the fear-obsessed frenzy expressed by the Inquisition, at the age of thirty-nine paused to pray before a statue of the crucified One and was swept by a tidal wave of longing to respond to the Divine love that had been so recklessly spilled upon her, the seed of the longing for the renewal of the church was planted in her heart. "What caused her," wrote the martyred German Jewish Carmelite philosopher, Edith Stein, "to realize the needs and demands of her time with such penetration? Precisely the fact . . . that she let herself be drawn even more deeply into the inner parts of her 'Interior Castle,' even unto that hidden chamber where He could say to her 'that it was time she took upon her His affairs as if they were her own, and that He would take her affairs upon Himself.' "[1] It is not for her work as a sixteenth-century Spanish convent reformer and founder with which she began, that we look to Teresa of Avila today, but rather because she saw and took upon herself the only enduring means for the renewal of a worldly church, namely, the renewal of its interior life, and in the course of it, that she left us treasures for exploring the interior life itself.

Today Protestant, Catholic, Quaker, we each stand alike in the same condition of desperate need. We do not need to emphasize the weight of the authority of the late Carl G. Jung to realize the truth of his words: "Whether from an intellectual, moral or aesthetic point of view, the undercurrents of the psychic life of the West are an uninviting picture. We have built a monumental world about us, and we have slaved for it with unequalled energy. But it is so imposing because we have spent upon the outside all that is imposing in our natures—and what we find when we look within must necessarily be as it is, shabby and insufficient."[2]

The late Arnold Toynbee, in his *An Historian Looks at Religion,*[3] points out that from the beginning of the seventeenth century to the present, the genius of the West has gone into technical and scientific discoveries accompanied by a highly naive neglect of the bent character of the world, of the lump of sin within men and women. Caught in the net of this terrible freedom, we must have a fresh surge of direction, or we perish. At the very point where Toynbee forsees a fresh burst of the investment of a much larger portion of our "liquid creativity," our "liquid spiritual capital," in the direction of the cultivation of the deepest religious life and insight, and the absolutely vital mobilization of our religious and educational resources to point them in this direction, we are instead being treated to a fresh deluge of the monotonous public voices of our time still fixed on what Toynbee calls "The Idolization of the Invincible Technician," crying out for more technicians, more engineers, and more physical scientists. They, and the vast foundation resources behind them, seem determined to meet our crisis by redoubling their efforts on the very scientific stereotypes that have accentuated our predicament. The late Dean Inge once noted that "Nothing fails like success" and we in our time seem bent on proving it.

In the midst of this desperate plight, we are concerned with the renewal of the interior life of Christian men and women in this generation. Teresa of Avila in her *Life* gives us the mandate of our open conspiracy. "I should be very glad, that as in these days men meet together to conspire against the Divine Majesty . . . so we five who at present love each other in Christ should also endeavor sometimes to meet together for the purpose of undeceiving each other, for conferring on the means of reforming ourselves, and of giving God the greatest pleasure."[4]

Protestantism and Spiritual Mediocrity

We cannot begin without the frankest of personal confession, first about the tradition in which we stand, and secondly about our calling, and ourselves. The Protestant religious tradition has had two areas where it was seriously "zuruckhaltend," dangerously shy. For the most part it has wistfully shied away from encouraging holiness and sanctity among its members and has been willing to settle for a middle spiritual condition, for a doctrine of "Nothing in excess." Leon Bloy's gibe about how in our day "Christians gallop with due moderation to martyrdom" or the description of a French disciple of his who declares that Christians "are dying of complacency and insipidity, of vulgarized and minimized truths, of a religion reduced to our standards" both seem off beat or at least provocations to defensive rebuttal as they come to our ears, and such a reaction is not untypical of contemporary Protestantism. This same Free Church tradition has consistently enough been equally suspicious and reluctant in acknowledging and being in a central way concerned about what history has shown to be the indispensable condition of real holiness, and sanctity, namely interior prayer and the price which it may exact from those who follow it.

In its theology at least, the classical Protestant tradition has insisted that God's grace was enough, that the act of salvation wrought in Jesus Christ was enough, that in man's condition of depravity, nothing but a major operation will suffice. In any case the Surgeon General must decide if and when that operation will take place, and whether the operation will occur under a total and not a local anaesthetic, thereby making the patient's part in the operation almost minimal. For four hundred years it has gloried in this objectivity, in the once-and-for-all-ness of the act of Christ. The fresh and moving rediscovery of this same accent in this generation has renewed this focus.

This tradition has known haltingly the Incarnation, faintly and mistrustfully the witness of the life of Jesus Christ himself, but fiercely and centrally the redemptive significance of the crucifixion. It has, however, paid little attention to the resurrection and the Holy Spirit, to Pentecost or to the personal and corporate response, in the way of a fierce loving response on the part of men and women to this matchless gift.

Lennart Segerstrole, who was Finland's greatest painter, once showed me a watercolor sketch that he was taking to a friend who was a most faithful State Church Christian in Helsinki. This man confessed that Christ had died to redeem his sin. He expected this to take care of his personal situation. He lived a decent life. But according to Lennart Segerstrole, there was in him no glint of joy, no hint of the good news, no terrible hunger for more of God at any price. It was a transactional situation. On the right side of the watercolor Segerstrole had in a few deft strokes sketched his friend lying prostrate and inert before the crucified Christ. On the left side, his prostrate body was again depicted, but now before it stood the risen Christ, arms outstretched and radiant with light, and rising up out of the full-length prostrate body of his friend, was a pneumatic body that leaned yearningly forward with an almost supernatural, El Greco-like eagerness to respond to the invitation given it by the radiant One who faced it.

Segerstrole seems to me to have sketched for us a dimension in Protestantism for which we inwardly yearn and whose authenticity we secretly do not doubt. Yet when the offensive labels of Pelagian, Platonistic, moralistic, self-obsessed, monastic, subjectivist, illuminist, enthusiastic, begin to rise, and when the traditional Wittenberg demand that "Grace is all" is hurled at us, we waver. Can we deny that German and British pietism, the Quakers, and the Anglican metaphysical poets of the seventeenth century—the very groups who have furnished us with much of the best Protestant devotional material which we possess—are not all assailable by one or another of these epithets? And as for the Roman Catholic devotional classics to which many Protestants have turned in their desperate and unfulfilled hunger for authentic spiritual encouragement, these are often enough under even sharper Protestant attack as overly concerned with personal growth in the life of devotion.

Is it, therefore, surprising that breathing the prayer "make no more giants Lord, but elevate the race," this Protestant tradition should be little given to the cultivation among its members of a yearning for sanctity, of a life in which God had more and more His undivided sway, or for the intensive cultivation of the conditions of that sanctity: interior prayer and its subsequent transformation of life?

Yet for all of this lukewarmness, we hunger. And we know well enough that there is a response. There is an answering back to the Grace of God on your part and on mine that is all-important. We know, too, that the redeeming of our time calls for nothing less than the blazing up out of our prostrate bodies of an authentic, original, passionate, interior life in answer to the Living Flame that confronts us.

When Georges Bernanos writes in his *Diary of a Country Priest* of the costly business of preaching the word, we know what he is talking about. He has de Torcy say:

> The word of God is a red-hot poker. And you had preach it 'ud
> go picking it up with a pair of tongs, for fear of burning yorself. You
> daren't get hold of it with both hands. It's too funny! Why the padre
> who descends from the pulpit of Truth, with a mouth like a hen's

vent, a little hot but pleased with himself, he's not been preaching: at best he's purring like a tabby cat. Mind you that can happen to us all, we're all half asleep, it's the devil to wake us up, sometimes—the apostles slept all right at Gethsemane. Still there's a difference . . . And mind there's many a fellow who waves his arms and sweats like a furniture remover isn't necessarily any more wakened than the rest. On the contrary I simply mean that when the Lord has drawn from me some word for the good of souls, I know because of the pain of it.

And he goes on later to add, "The word of God! 'Give me back my word,' the Judge will say on the last day. When you think what certain people will have to unpack on that occasion, its no laughing matter, I assure you."[5]

Yet it is not so much a fear of the price, of the pain that the word "for the good of souls" would cost that brings those in the ministry to despair. It is a deeper fear that perhaps they are so outwardly involved and so inwardly dispersed, so "cut off outside ourselves" that even if that word should come on our lips, it would lack the authenticity, lack the authority to carry it to its mark. For how can we who are ourselves inwardly numb speak to the condition of congregations made up of those who are caught up and held magnetized by the same fields of force that have numbed us, their clergy? We must ourselves be open to a more powerful magnet in order to release them from the power of the one in which they stand. Again and again there comes the realization that the liberator must himself be liberated, that the mediocre minister is an ugly thing, that this kind of possession cometh not out except by prayer and fasting, and that souls all about us are waiting to come into birth, waiting to be drawn to a deeper answering back to God, but that we ourselves are not yet ready, we are not able to bear them now.

John of the Cross speaks about the window through which the light of the word must come, about the life behind the sermon. "The exercise of the preaching, he says, "is spiritual rather than vocal. For although it is practiced by means of outward words, its power and efficacy reside not in these but in the inward spirit. It is a common matter that so far as we can judge here below, the better the life of the preacher, the greater fruit it produces."[6]

Ministers of the gospel have many occupational hazards and diseases and these have frequently been diagnosed with telling power. But all too seldom have the ministers been reminded of the unmatched spiritual opportunity that has been almost uniquely lavished on them by God, namely the opportunity of being confronted hour after hour with human problems that are utterly beyond their own strength to unravel, and which drive them back to listen for, and to draw upon a deeper wisdom and strength than they are able in themselves to supply. How often are ministers drawn back into the supernatural life of God, back into what Tauler calls "suffering in God" by their own weakness and the sheer abysmal personal needs of those who call on them for help?

"What Then Is a Real Man of Prayer?"

When Evelyn Underhill once sketched for a group of ministers what their calling demanded that they become and continue to be, she was quite naturally compelled to describe a man of prayer who might well be an inconspicuous member of the congregation.

> What then is a real man of prayer? He is one who deliberately wills and steadily desires that his intercourse with God and other souls shall be controlled and activated at every point by God Himself; one who has so far developed and educated his spiritual sense, that his supernatural environment is more real and solid to him than his natural environment. A man of prayer is not necessarily a man who says a number of offices, or abounds in detailed intercessions; but he is a child of God who is and knows himself to be in the deeps of his soul attached to God, and is wholly and entirely guided by the Creative Spirit of his prayer and work. This is not merely a bit of pious language. It is a description as real and concrete as I can make it, of the only real apostolic life. Every Christian starts with a chance of it; but only a few develop it. The laity distinguish in a moment the clergy who have it from the clergy who have it not: there is nothing that you can do for God, or for the souls of men, which exceeds in importance the achievement of that spiritual temper and attitude.[7]

Is there any less costly way than the way Evelyn Underhill has described to minister either to the needs of persons caught up in our society where we are "distracted from distraction, by distraction" or to the needs of the swollen technological body of our society? If there is a cheaper way, our Christian history does not reveal it. Whether it is a soul in inner torment or a society walking along a parapet with cosmic arson ten stories below, it is only one who is attached to God and in the flood of His power, who can witness convincingly to what alone can answer to the muffled yearning in the human heart.

For Giving Me Desire

What, then, is this way of sanctity, this power of holiness, that can speak in us today? To what are we called? It is to nothing short of a life of attention to and abandonment to the besieging love of God. When God says to the soul, "*You must learn to pay attention,*" he is speaking of the deinsulation of the human soul that must take place in order for the soul to be made aware of its situation, and leads first of all to a querying of who we are.

At the close of a powerful prose soliloquy written in a Nazi prison that he was never to leave, Dietrich Bonhoeffer—having canvassed at length whether he is the bold knight of Christian courage that his family and friends and jailers think him to be, or whether he is just the lonely, caged, faint-hearted one that he knows himself to be— concludes with the lines:

> Who am I? This or the other?
> Am I one person today and tomorrow another?
> Am I both at once? A hypocrite before others
> And before myself a contemptible woe-begone weakling?
> Or is something within me still like a beaten army,
> Fleeing in disorder from a victory already achieved,
> Who am I? They mock me these lonely questions of mine.
> Whoever I am, Thou knowest Oh God, I am Thine.[8]

In the closing line, the above surface cry of us all: "Who am I" gives way to the muted question, the real human question "*Whose* am I," and there is no equivocation in Bonhoeffer's answer "Thou knowest O God, I am Thine."

This is the deep stifled cry of the human heart. This is what Thomas Traherne tried to describe in his beautiful sonnet called "Desire."

For giving me desire,
An eager thirst, a burning ardent fire,
A virgin infant flame,
A Love with which into the world I came,
An inward hidden heavenly love,
Which in my soul did work and move,
And ever me inflame
With restless longing, heavenly avarice,
That never could be satisfied,
That did incessantly a Paradise
Unknown suggest, and something undescried
Discern, and bear me to it; be
Thy Name for ever praised by me.[9]

It is this same yearning that the seventeenth-century poet George Herbert spoke of in *The Pulley* where, after prodigally pouring into man blessing after blessing, God stays his hand and holds back the gift of rest that if all other means fail, then "If goodness lead him not, yet weariness may tosse him to My breast."[10]

Now true sanctity does not mean the pharisaical pretensions to righteousness of the religiously complacent. No one knows more profoundly than those who venture into this life of sanctity how ridden with still-to-be-redeemed areas their lives remain. Nor does it mean that they try to assume some standardized pattern of life that has come to be associated with this life, whether the pattern is to enter some "religious" vocation, or some "religious" community, or to try to emulate some personality type that sanctity is conceived to follow. A leafing through of the pages of Schamoni's *The Face of the Saints*,[11] where he has collected the paintings, drawings, and photographs of some of those who have been publicly acknowledged as belonging to this company, is enough to reveal what an infinite diversity of temperaments and personal types there were among them.

What Bloy means by being a saint is in terms of a life that is ever more recklessly responding to the primal human query *"Whose* Am I?", "To Whom Do I Belong?" In these terms, sanctity means simply a growing willingness, or a growing willingness to be made willing, to be open to this tide of redemptive love that besieges the soul when it is confronted by Christ. It is nothing more or less than letting God have more and more his undivided sway in our hearts. To this *"Whose*

Am I?" the deeply buried yearning for sanctity is expressed in the degree of my readiness to reply "Whoever I am, Thou knowest O God, I am Thine."

But the life of sanctity is not simply a life of desire, of yearning, of hunger, of thirst. These according to the New Testament are a necessary condition of attention to God. "Blessed are those who hunger and thirst after righteousness, for they shall be filled." "Woe unto the rich for they already have their reward." But hunger although necessary is never in itself a sufficient condition. The sufficiency is supplied by the redemptive life of the living God, poured out in Jesus Christ, and poured out in each moment here and now. The life of sanctity is a mad response to the initiative of the mad love of God that has come into a realization that God holds it in the utter consuming, transforming, energizing irradiation of His costly love.

Eckhart puts it so clearly: "God is foolishly in love with us. It seems He has forgotten heaven and earth and diety; his entire business seems to be with me alone, to give me everything to comfort me; he gives it to me suddenly. He gives it to me wholly, he gives it to me perfect, he gives it all the time, and he gives it to all creatures."[12] The person who is moving into this life is not bent on a deeper interior life. He is not bent on a life of sanctity. He is not his own disciple. These are all short circuits of a shallow sort. He is bent on God; drawn toward God; in a state of profound repentance about the inadequacy of his life, yet with a reckless sense of gratitude to one who can draw him, even him, shadows and all, toward the light.

The Hiddenness of Sanctity

Now because sanctity, because this interior life is the side effect of this attention, adherence, attachment of the soul to God, it can never be described directly. From the outside, those in whom God is more and more having His way look just as others do. There is even a kind of cloak of ordinariness about them. To be sure there are clues. One does not need to go as far as Kierkegaard does in his famous figure of the Knight of Faith in *Fear and Trembling,* who on the outside looks exactly like any butcher's assistant and who on his way home along the Strandvej in Copenhagen has his surface thought on the good supper that he knows his wife is preparing for him, yet who on the inside behind this stage drop of anonymous ordinariness has yielded all to God and lives from moment to moment in abject dependence upon God, treading on the 70,000 fathoms of water. The incognito is rarely as complete as this.

There is a story of Albert Schweitzer riding in a roomette on the train from New York to Chicago on his way to the Goethe Festival at Aspen, Colorado in 1949. Two women were passing by and seeing this distinguished head, the more brazen of the two stopped before the open door and asked, "Do I have the honor to be speaking to . . . Albert Einstein?" Schweitzer, his Alsatian peasant humor thoroughly taking in the situation, replied, "No, Madame, our heads look very much alike on the outside but they are very different on the inside," and then asked her if she did not want Albert Einstein's authograph and wrote on a slip "Albert Einstein, by his friend Albert Schweitzer." The head of the saint, too, looks very much the same as anyone else's on the outside, but how different it is on the inside. "The little more and how much it is. The little less and what worlds away."

Coventry Patmore has gathered this up in a classic passage where in speaking of sanctity, he writes:

> You may live in the same house with him and never find out . . . He will give you an agreeable impression of his general inferiority to yourself. You must not, however, presume upon this inferiority so far as to offer him any affront, for he will be sure to answer you with some quite unexpected remark, showing a presence of mind— arising I suppose from the presence of God—which will make you feel that you have struck rock and only shaken your own shoulder. If you compel him to speak about religion . . . He will most likely dwell with reiteration on commonplaces with which you were perfectly well acquainted before you were twelve years old; but you must make allowance for him, and remember that the knowledge which is to you a superficies is to him solid . . . I once asked a person to tell me the real difference. The reply was that the saint does everything that any decent person does, only somewhat better and with a totally different motive.[13]

This "grace of doing common things in a supernatural way" eludes measure yet it is rarely completely cloaked. Who has not at some point felt it and been drawn to what it reveals when he encounters it?

The Grand Canyon and the Interior Life

Difficult as it may be to describe this interior life, the quality of sanctity and holiness in life, there are a few features that seem to be constants within it. In the first place the irradiation of the person by Divine Grace and the focus of attention upon God has not left the life as it was. The epistle notes that "For Christ did not please himself" (Romans 4:3) and in this there has always been a clue to the availability of those who have seemed to be inwardly joined to His company.

Our family once visited three of the great American national wonders—Bryce Canyon, Zion National Park, and the Grand Canyon. Geologists tell us that these three regions represent three different geological ages. Bryce Canyon is the youngest and the soft sandstone of its surface rock has been cut by the elements into the fantastic shapes that cast their spell on visitors. The rock formations at Zion are in a geologically middle-aged situation where nearly all of the sandstone has long since been worn away and where the great open flat surfaces of the hard rock masses are exposed. The Grand Canyon reveals the oldest level of all, where over the ages the action of water, wind, and frost has long ago dissolved away the sandstone, and has even worn through the heavy rock masses still to be seen at Zion, until only a clean unobstructed chasm remains, open without resistance to the wind and to the sun to sweep through as they will.

There seems in this experience to be found some clue to the interior life of sanctity. For in the seasoned man of God, we begin to see the open expendable character of this mature third level. He is still himself: unique, individual, no man's copy. Yet so much of the nonessential self has been worn away until he is God's and God is his and he gets on with the day's business with a spontaneity and freshness that is not wholly lost on anything he does.

Of course there are the waverings, the "night shifts," the dark nights of the soul when still another rock layer is being undermined and prepared to be avalanched and swept into the valley for God's disposal. No one is spared that. Emma Hausknecht died in the summer of 1956. It would be hard to name anyone outside of Albert Schweitzer in the period since the present Lambarené hospital was constructed in 1925 who is to be credited with holding it together against the massed destructive gravitational forces that are always pulling it apart. I remember coming into my tiny cell-like room in the guest quarters there one late afternoon. The moist equatorial heat of that day was enough to wilt the stoutest heart. There I found Emma Hausknecht breathlessly engaged in moving me to a still smaller cubicle because some timber merchant and his wife had suddenly appeared to spend several days at the hospital. My appearance there as she struggled with the awkwardly hung mosquito net over my bed was the last straw, and she cried out a torrent of defiance, "Why do I stay down here in this terrible place? Why day after day and year after year do I stagger from one annoyance to another? Why am I such a fool?" I could only answer, "I think I know why you stay," and it was enough. "Yes, of course, I know too," and there was nothing more to say. There is a wise saying that it is not falling in the water that drowns a man, but staying in.

Teresa of Avila, journeying as usual in her wagon with the curtained top, was determined to get on to Burgos even if it did meaning crossing the flooded river Arlanzon on an improvised bridge of pontoon floats that were swimming in water. When the carriage toppled over and forced her to wade to shore in water halfway up her legs, she cried out, "Lord amid so many ills, this comes on top of all the rest," and then she heard the Lord say to her, "That is how I treat my friends," and the message drew from her the tart reply, "Ah my God, that is why you have so few of them!" But flare up as she would, she is soon back in the deep cut groove, back in Grand Canyon country again with her, "Oh God, we thank you for the bad roads," and, "Thank you, dear Lord, for the fleas."[14]

Francis de Sales, who freely admits that self-love in us never dies as long as we live, is not kept by this fact from his knees and from his classic prayer, "Yes, God, Yes, and always Yes."

There is a line of G. K. Chesterton's which says "And the heart of man is a heavy load for a man to bear along." He might have said "for a man to bear *alone.*" For the man of an interior life, from all the evidences, also has his days of "low visibility" when his attention is dispersed and he forgets that he does not bear his heart alone. But the man of interior life knows the way back into the castle again, the way to become a child again. "The greatest as well as the least," wrote Isaac Penington, "must be daily taught of the Lord in ascending and descending or they will miss the way." These are the words of an old veteran who knows that in yielding to God there is no guarantee of continuous infallibility. There is no insurance against opaqueness. It is simply a business of starting all over again every day and every hour of the day, and doing it all so naturally that it usually escapes outer notice. No, the availability of the life is not the same in those who are veterans on this way.

Not to be Safe but to be Faithful

There is another characteristic that seems to mark the Grand Canyonites. They never seem to be spared from troubles, but only to look at trouble through different eyes. The Kikuyu Christians experiencing martyrdom for their faith at the hands of the Mau Mau prayed, "Oh Lord we ask Thee not to be safe, but to be faithful." It is as though these testing ones had already been plunged to the bottom of where trouble comes from, as though they had already faced the most horrible fear that could be conjured up, as though they, too, had died and descended into hell, perhaps had had an extended period of residence there, but that now they knew a joy which this horrible darkness not only could never penetrate but went about living as though it would one day be reabsorbed into its ocean of light. Now they were so difficult to shake because there was nothing more to see. These living in this spirit would seem to affirm William Russell Maltby's insistence that Jesus promised those who would follow him only three things: that they should be "absurdly happy, entirely fearless, and always in trouble."

A story is told of a child of three visiting his aunt and begging at night for the hall light to be left on and his bedroom door to be kept ajar. Reminded that he never was afraid of the dark when he was at home, he responded, "Yes, but there it's *my* dark." These men and women have seemed to have had their own dark, their well-domesticated troubles, torn from them and to have been compelled to live even in cosmic darkness until they found a light that darkness could obscure but never extinguish.

In the closing scene of Alan Paton's *Cry the Beloved Country* where the old Umfundisi is on his knees in the fateful dawn when they are hanging his son on the Johannesburg prison scaffold, there is again the power of God's caring for black and white alike that rises in his heart. The trouble is not removed. The innocent white man his son had murdered is dead. His son has been executed. The pain remains. It will be with him always. But now, while nothing outwardly has changed, yet all is reversed. He does not bear his heavy heart alone. Now what was on the right is on the left and what was on the left is on the right. It is the same, and yet all is different.[15]

There is a translation from a little Japanese book that is called *A Gentleman in Prison.*[16] It tells the story of a murderer who during his stay in prison felt the compassion of Christ drive through his heart like a hard, blunt-pointed nail, and like the penitent thief on the cross, nothing mattered after that. The inevitable execution took place but not before he had shared with all who met him this wave of caring for men and women of all conditions.

I know a Norwegian pastor who was arrested for his share in the underground, and after a trial in Germany was sentenced to death and who, by a series of extraordinary events, was still among the living when the war ground to a close in 1945. I once asked him what happens inside a man when a sentence of death is passed upon him. He could only speak for himself, he replied, but for him, it was an occasion when a great flood of heavenly mercy poured into his heart: for his judges, for his captors, for the Norwegian Quislings, for his countrymen, for all men everywhere. It was a mercy so clean that he regretted his own death only because he would no longer be about to try to change the hearts of men at the war's close to help them to make their decisions in this all-encompassing climate of compassion.

The Jewish philosopher Paul-Louis Landsberg, whose honest mind could never be persuaded that the classical philosophical arguments against suicide were other than intellectually specious and who in his flight into France carried a vial of poison to make away with himself if he should fall into the hands of the Nazis and face torture, fell first, as his destiny would have it, into the hand of Christ. Knowing that the Gestapo prison was his inevitable destination, he threw away his poison vial, this swift way out, reconstructed his philosophy in the light of the One to whom he abandoned all, and died as he anticipated in a Nazi prison in Germany, leaving us one of the most moving books on Christian abandonment in connection with the problem of death and suicide that any generation has ever received.[17] With one voice, this company then could say with Simone Weil, "If we want a love that will protect the soul from wounds, we must love something other than God."[18]

These long looks into the abyss dare to see what is there, dare to love without the help of anything on earth, and they inwardly reauthenticate by their personal appropriation of them, the Psalmist's words, "Whom have I in heaven but Thee, and there is none on earth that I desire beside thee. My heart and my flesh faileth, but God is the strength of my heart and my portion forever" (Psalm 73:25–26)". They give us a clue to a second aspect of the interior life of sanctity.

Somehow We Get Along

Closely allied to this business of having encountered what they are most afraid of and found One who had been there first, is the willingness of these persons to take life as it comes and instead of defending themselves against those who attack them, to disclose their gift for joining the staff of the prosecuting attorney who is proceeding against them in court. They have even been known to point out to the jury how much more damaging material there is against them than the prosecutor has even begun to uncover. Who could have given his enemies more shells for their arsenal than Augustine in his *Confessions* with his documented accounts of his youthful excesses, his lies and trickery with his mother, his fierce ambition and pride? But how little any of this mattered to Augustine, if it could encourage one other man not to give up hope that what God's mercy could do for a rogue like Augustine, he might also do for him. Teresa of Avila, when she heard of an attack on her character, gaily consoled her friend, "They do me the greatest possible good, for if I am not guilty of what they accuse me of, I have offended God on so many other occasions that the one pays for another."[19]

In 1948 when Germany was still a shambles, I once heard two educators describing their institutions. A head of a French school at le Chambon told of what a beautiful spirit reigned in his school, how the faculty were of a common mind and commitment, the students ardent and so eager for what was given them that they were willing to put in holidays and extra hours to help build desperately needed buildings for the school. Then a grizzled old German woman stood up. The Nazis had first driven her out of Germany and she had gone to Denmark where she had set up a school, and when Denmark was invaded she fled, this time to England, where she had worked as a teacher. As soon as the authorities would permit her in 1946, she returned to a starving Germany in order to reopen the Odenwald School. She stood there frail and battered as she began her remarks—with wistful praise for the model school she had just heard described. She remarked on how wonderful it must be to teach in such an exemplary institution. Her school, she assured us, was exactly the opposite. The faculty of teachers was made up of everything from Communists to Barthians who were at each other's throats from morning until night. The student body was hungry most of the time and full of every known aftermath of the various war neuroses. The equipment was terrible; the pay miserable; the hours and student teacher load quite impossible. "But," she added, significantly, "Somehow, I can't explain it, in spite of all this, we get along!"

Dorothy Day's talks on the ghastly collection of social and personal misfits that made up the Catholic Worker movement and the incredible troubles they encountered in trying to carry on, always seemed to end on the same note. "But, somehow, we get along!" There is in these people very little sense of pride, of self-preservation, of self-conceal-ment, and they can ridicule and laugh at themselves and at their enterprises with wholehearted merriness that restores to its rightful place in life what heavenly humor was meant to be.

Tertullian declares that "the Christian saint is hilarious," hinting at the fact that to be really happy about anything you have to be happy about everything, and Teresa of Avila prayed to be delivered from sour, vinegary Christians. These, however, only bring us to the thresh-old of a closely related mark of this life: the presence of Christian joy. Von Hügel took great pains to single out this demand in the qualifica-tions for canonization. There must be ample evidence not only of heroism, but of the presence of Christian joy. Yet this joy is as mysteri-ous and as unfathomable as the character of sanctity itself, and like sanctity and holiness it seems never to have been the goal, but only the byproduct of the soul's attachment to God.

Joy is such an utterly different category from pleasure or the ab-sence of pain. It is a quivering needle between the soul's utter satisfac-tion and its contrary sense of its own bent toward nothingness, between what Simone Weil so subtly calls *Grace* and its natural countering downthrust *Gravity*. To "weep for joy" is ever so natural because joy lies both between and beyond both tears and laughter. Yet there is a great lightening of the heart in it and a healing that knows no equal. To a heart that has known its balm, there can be the merriness of the scaffold itself of a Thomas More who asks the Lord Lieutenant to help him up the ladder with the genial "and as for my coming down, let me shift for myself."

Here is something beyond good and evil. It is here that Meister Eckhart's joyous beggar who, on being wished a good morrow, declares "I never had an ill one;" it is here that Francis of Assisi in the *Little Flowers* can describe the incredible buffetings attending on perfect joy; it is here that we make up the sufferings found in Christ, and do it with the midnight hymns of a Paul and Silas singing in their prison chains. "Nothing," and that means *Nothing* "can separate us from the love of Christ."

Kindlers and the Purifiers of the Dream

Is it any wonder, then, that persons who have experienced the rare detachment brought about by Christian joy should often see things upside down as far as contemporary public acceptances are concerned, and yet have their vision marked by a terrible logic of elementary simplicity when its real measure is taken? Often only very simple people offer any analogy to the perceptive powers of the saint who sees with noonday vision. In South Africa I dined one day with an African evangelist who had been blind from birth. He described to me how, when he was a boy, his parents and his friends began keeping him from sitting here, from standing there, from riding here and from eating there and explained only that these were out of bounds for Blacks. He insisted that as a blind man he simply could not understand what this was all about. Men were not all alike to him. But the only real differentiation he could find was that they were either kind and considerate, or rough and inconsiderate. What had color to do with this? His directness, like that of the saints, raises the question as to who, after all, is really blind in the world? Is it society, or is it this man?

Francis of Assisi with his principle of Franciscan shame turned upside down the usual judgment that those who are poor and in want probably have been improvident and deserve their status and should be ashamed of themselves and of their condition, while those in plenty may be proud that they have only received what they deserved. Francis declared that when he, a follower of Christ, finds any man who has less than he has, not the impoverished one, but he himself, is swept with shame and with a longing to meet that man's need. What madness, yet what sanity!

Is it, then, any reason for drastic surprise that out of this life of sanctity have come impulses of such cleanness that the world is again and again purged at its heart and society is renewed from within by these fresh and astonishing interpretations of its dream, of that for which in its heart of hearts, it yearns if it only dared openly to acknowledge it. In spite of all the reservations we may wish to add, it is hard to see in any other light the poultice-like power of Schweitzer's clean act upon the conscience of his generation. In his life he turned the tables upside down, and men have gone about their own jobs differently because he dared to act as he did and set off a chain reaction of human concern.

When a man like Arthur Shearly Cripps, whose poems you can read in the *Oxford Book of Mystical Verse,* left a respectable berth first in England, and then in Southern Rhodesian society, in order to throw in his lot with the Africans, live in a rondavel four days' walk from the capital city, and share the Africans' degraded status in a longing in some way to balance the budget, something happened in Southern Africa whose implications are still at work. I once asked a Matabele statesman how the Africans looked upon Arthur Cripps, after a long pause to ponder the matter, he replied, "I think they loved him more than they loved themselves."

On Longing to Dare and Daring

I do not know how better to express this longing to dare, but not daring, which marks our stooped world and the stooped souls of those who dwell in it than to cite the closing scene in Laurens Van der Post's *Bar of Shadow* where, with the war over and the Tokyo War Crimes Court verdict completed, a Japanese officer awaits execution for his brutalities as head of a prison camp. He is visited in his death cell by an English officer who has been both the victim and the witness of this

Japanese jailer's cruel attempt to carry out his Japanese military code ideal of patriotic fervor. In spite of all, he is deeply attached to this doomed Japanese, and as he tries to say good-bye to him, he is met by a wide grin.

Van der Post writes:

> But the eyes, Lawrence said, were not laughing. There was a light in them of a moment which transcends lesser moments wherein all earthly and spiritual conflicts tend to be resolved and unimportant, all partiality and incompletion gone, and only a deep somber between-night-and morning glow left. It transformed Hara's strange distorted features. . . . He was so moved by it, by the expression in those Archaic eyes that he wanted to turn back into the cell. Indeed he tried to go back but something would not let him. Half of himself, a deep instinctive, natural, impulsive half, wanted to go back, clasp Hara in his arms, kiss him good-bye on the forehead, and say, "We may not be able to stop and undo the hard old wrongs of the great world outside, but through you and me no evil shall come either in the unknown to which you are going, or in this imperfect and haunted dimension of awareness through which I move. Thus between us, we shall cancel out all private and personal evil, thus arrest the private and personal consequences to blind action and reaction, thus prevent specifically the general incomprehension and misunderstanding, hatred and revenge of our time from spreading further." But the words would not be uttered, and half of him, the conscious half of the officer at the door with a critical alert sentry at his side held him powerless on the threshold. So for the last time the door shut on Hara and his golden grin.[20]

The difference between Lawrence, who stands for us all in his longing to dare, but not daring, and the man of interior life, is that what we yearn to do and shrink from, he does. Fastidiousness goes, invisible lines disappear, and the spontaneous embrace that melts the ice in the heart of the world is given.

Someone has defined an optimist as a man who, when the preacher says, "And finally," begins to put on his coat. Without extending an instant invitation to any such optimistic gesture on your part, the time has nevertheless come to draw this chapter to a close. I remember a story of a group of Quakers who had gone camping together in Canada. After a long day's trip by canoe, much of which had been made in the rain, they were shiveringly trying to get a fire going, and sent all hands out to gather wood. After a long struggle with the wet wood, the fire builder had at last gotten a frail little blaze going when one of the company staggered in toward the group bearing a huge log and promptly dropped it on the flickering fire with an exultant "Look what I've brought!" and effectively put out the fire.

The Sanity of Sanctity

In trying to depict the character of the interior life, my account of its doglike character may have had the opposite of a kindling effect. But the 10,000-mile journey begins with the first step, and one of the most impressive things about these seasoned pilgrims we have been keeping company with here is their vast sanity. When her male companions had seemed to make the interior life available only to those in one station or one temperament or to place it at the conclusion of some arduous climb up Everest, Teresa of Avila chided them, and even teased them a little. God's grace is sufficient for all conditions. "It would cost us dear not to seek for God until we were dead to the world. Mary Magdalen was not, when she found him, nor the woman of Samaria, nor the Canaanites."[21] She even went as far as to declare, "God preserve me from people who are so spiritual that, come what may, they want to turn everything into a perfect contemplation," or to sigh as she prayed, "From silly devotions, Oh Lord, deliver us." The last thing to be desired is some kind of hothouse religiosity; and Teresa might even have given a blessing to the old Muslim who declared "The true saint goes in and out amongst the people and eats and sleeps with them and buys and sells in the market and marries and takes part in social intercourse and never forgets God for a single moment," provided that the accent upon the final clause in this sentence is not overlooked. For Teresa it is always the same note: "The highest perfection does not consist in interior joys, nor in sublime raptures, nor in visions, nor in having the gift of prophecy, but in bringing our will into such conformity with the will of God, that whatever we know He desires, that also shall we desire with our whole affection." And this condition can begin anywhere, in anyone, in any station, for the soul of each man is forever under God's siege.

On Coming Still Further In

There is, however, one final trait that marks the interior life wherever it is found. There is no record of it ever growing in those who do not know prayer. The rule is almost as blunt as that: No prayer, no interior life. And we have no record of a saint who did not pray, or of real growth in the interior life that is not marked by this inner yielding, this inner attention to God.

There is no way out around this inner yielding which is at the heart of prayer. And those who take this way begin with themselves. They give the world back to God beginning with themselves. Importunate as the New Testament account of the man begging for bread for his family or the widow before the judge; slow and unspectacular, yet willing to pray not on one knee only but on both knees, this is the hidden life that can alone renew the church in our time.

There is a line of Sidney Lanier's that knows our generation almost better than it knows itself.

> Oh age that half believest, thou half believest
> Half doubtest the substance of thine own half doubt,
> And half perceivest what thou half perceivest
> Standest at thy temple door heart in, head out.

To those who would renew the church in our time, the answering voice calls out, "Come in, come in, come still further in."

Notes

1. Quoted in Hilda C. Graef, *The Scholar and the Cross* (London: Longman, 1955).
2. *Modern Man in Search of a Soul* (New York: Harcourt, Brace, 1933), p. 125.
3. *An Historian Looks at Religion* (New York: Oxford, 1956), see chapters 17 and 20.
4. *Life,* translated by Allison Peers (London: Sheed and Ward, 1944), Chapter 16, p. 99.
5. *Diary of a Country Priest,* translated by Pamela Morris (London: John Lane, 1937), pp. 64–5, 70.

6. Bede Frost, *John of the Cross* (New York: Harpers, 1927), p. 17.
7. *Concerning the Inner Life* (London: Methuen, 1926), p. 14.
8. *The Cost of Discipleship* (London: S.C.M., 1959), p. 15.
9. *Poetical Works* (London: Do Bell, 1906) p. 119.
10. *Oxford Book of English Mystical Verse* (London: Oxford, 1916), pp. 28–29.
11. *The Face of the Saints* (New York: Pantheon, 1942).
12. *Meister Eckhart,* translated by C. de B. Evans (London: John Watkins, 1924) p. 231.
13. *From the Rod, the Root and the Flower,* quoted in E. Herman, *Creative Prayer* (New York: Harper, 1934) p. 109.
14. Marcelle Auclair, *St. Theresa of Avila* (London: Burns & Oates, 1953) p. 391.
15. *Cry the Beloved Country* (New York: Scribners, 1948).
16. *A Gentleman in Prison,* translated by Caroline MacDonald (New York: Dovan, 1922).
17. *Death and Suicide* (London: Rockcliff, 1953).
18. *Gravity and Grace* (London: Routledge & Kegan Paul, 1952) p. xxii.
19. *Auclair,* p. 330.
20. L. Van der Post, *The Bar of Shadow* (New York: Morrow, 1956), pp. 58–9.
21. *Auclair,* p. 310.